Destination Z

All the events predicted in this book are educated guesses about what might happen in the business world over the next decade, written from the historical perspective of the year 2008 as though those events had already happened. The author has had no special access to information about any of the companies mentioned, but has extrapolated a variety of different scenarios from information already in the public domain at the time of writing. It is not intended that any reader should place any reliance whatsoever on any prediction or other statement made in this book. The author and publisher of this book disclaim any responsibility whatsoever for any consequences of such reliance.

Destination Z:
The History of the Future

Robert Baldock

JOHN WILEY & SONS
Chichester • New York • Weinheim • Brisbane • Singapore • Toronto

Copyright © 1999 John Wiley & Sons Ltd,
Baffins Lane, Chichester,
West Sussex PO19 1UD, England

National   01243 779777
International   (+44) 1243 779777
e-mail (for orders and customer service enquiries):
cs-books@wiley.co.uk
Visit our Home Page on http://www.wiley.co.uk
or http://www.wiley.com

Other Wiley Editorial Offices

John Wiley & Sons, Inc., 605 Third Avenue,
New York, NY 10158-0012, USA

WILEY-VCH Verlag GmbH, Pappelallee 3,
D-69469 Weinheim, Germany

Jacaranda Wiley Ltd, 33 Park Road, Milton,
Queensland 4064, Australia

John Wiley & Sons (Canada) Ltd, 22 Worcester Road,
Rexdale, Ontario M9W 1L1, Canada

John Wiley & Sons (Asia) Pte Ltd, Clementi Loop #02-01,
Jin Xing Distripark, Singapore 129809

Library of Congress Cataloging-in-Publication Data

Baldock, Robert, 1955–
    Destination Z : the history of the future / Robert Baldock.
        p.   cm.
    Includes bibliographical references and index.
    ISBN 0-471-98462-0 (cloth : alk. paper)
    1. Economic forecasting.   2. Business forecasting.
    3. Technological innovations—Economic aspects.   4. Twenty-first
century—Forecasts.   I. Title.
    HB3730.B265   1998
    658.4'0355—dc21   98–35070
                                                            CIP

British Library Cataloguing in Publication Data

A catalogue record for this book is available from the British Library

ISBN 0 471-98462-0

Typeset in 11 on 16pt Plantin by Mackreth Media Services, Hemel Hempstead
Printed and bound in Great Britain by Biddles Ltd, Guildford and King's Lynn.
This book is printed on acid-free paper responsibly manufactured from sustainable
forestry, in which at least two trees are planted for each one used in paper production.

To Doreen, Christopher and Danielle
My Future

Several major forces of change, each with the power of a tornado, are heading your way.

> Want to know what these are?
> If so, read chapters one and two

You cannot predict when these forces will hit your company or what the consequences will be.

> Not convinced the future is unpredictable?
> Then read chapters three to eight

Your boss has just walked into your office and asked you to prepare a five-year plan setting out, amongst other things, revenue forecasts by product/service/geography. How are you going to do this when so many people in your position have failed to make accurate predictions?

> Concerned?
> Then definitely read chapter nine as well

Finally, if you want to have fun while you plan your future, play Destination Z.

> Interested?
> Then read Appendix A before you pass the book on

Contents

Acknowledgements

A S YOU MIGHT EXPECT THERE ARE NUMEROUS PEOPLE I REALLY ought to thank for making this book possible. To name them all would be impractical so I will concentrate instead on three people who helped me the most—Sean Baenen, Tim Hindle and Markku Koppinen.

Markku was the Andersen Consulting manager who acted as the project manager on the scenario planning project that created the scenarios that are the main feature of this book. Markku deserves a special mention since he has continued to help me with this book long after he stopped being my project manager.

Sean used to work with Andersen Consulting and played a special role in helping us with the application of the scenario planning technique, being an expert on the subject. Sean played a major role in devising the stories that bring to life our scenarios. Shortly after doing this work for me, Sean decided to join the world's foremost firm of scenario planners—GBN—who also played a key role in our project. I am indebted to Sean (and GBN) for his continued help with this book.

Finally, but not least, I must thank Tim. When I decided to write this book I looked around for a writer to work with me. I recognised I had neither the time, nor the necessary talent to do it myself (business reports I can write with my eyes closed, but a book . . .). I happened upon Tim and I am extremely pleased I did because Tim did more than just turn existing material and my thoughts into this book. Over the many months that we worked together he went from being a transcriber to a major contributor. Tim, many, many thanks.

I really hope this book excites you, perhaps even worry you a little but also give you some thoughts about how you can shape our future.

Robert Baldock

About the Author

ROBERT BALDOCK IS A SENIOR PARTNER IN ANDERSEN Consulting, the world's leading management and technology consultancy. He joined the firm in 1976, in London at the age of 21 and became a partner in 1987, thus becoming one of the youngest people to ever make partner in the firm.

His first consulting assignment took him to the USA for nine months and although most of his work has since been in the UK, he has travelled extensively, acting in an advisory capacity to Andersen Consulting teams and clients across the globe. While the vast majority of his time has been spent working in the financial services industry, Mr Baldock has worked in a whole range of other consumer serving industries, including government, health care, retailing, utilities, oil and gas and motor racing.

Within Andersen Consulting he has built up a reputation for being a thought leader and innovator. He was responsible for leading a group of partners in Andersen's global financial services practice in developing a set of scenarios for the future of the financial services industry. The subsequent paper and futuristic video produced as a result of this work—'Virtualisation: The Future of Financial Services'—has been highly acclaimed both within and outside of the firm. Mr Baldock has held a number of positions within Andersen Consulting where he has been responsible for developing ideas and solutions to help Andersen's clients leapfrog their competition. He is particularly pleased with the work he completed in conjunction with the Nationwide Building Society, which led to the creation of the world's first virtual branch in 1995. Not only did this system exceed its business case; it also led to both organisations receiving multiple, prestigious awards including one from the Smithsonian Institute.

He is a regular speaker at conferences, and has written many papers and articles for trade magazines.

He is married, with two children and lives in London when he is not 30,000 feet above the ground. Apart from his family, his main passion is motor racing. He arranged Andersen's sponsorship of the Williams Formula 1 team and acts in an advisory capacity to the team.

Executive Summary—
Destination Z: The History Of
The Future

WHEN I BEGAN MY CAREER WITH ANDERSEN CONSULTING just over 20 years ago there was no such thing as a fax machine, a photocopier, a mobile phone or a PC. Typists tapped away noisily day in, day out, working on tasks that today take one-tenth of the time. Foreign phone calls had to be booked hours in advance with an operator, and by the time the call had been connected someone else might have won the business!

Since then there has been more change in the workplace than in any comparable period in history. Whatever industry we work in, we have had to learn and unlearn skills and habits at a rapid rate. And there are no signs of that rate abating.

Take the example of just one industry—banking, an industry that I know well—to see what a revolution has taken place over the past 20 years. In the 1970s, to join a big commercial bank as a trainee manager was to gain one of the safest 'jobs for life' on the market. The job involved a lot of personal contact with customers—customers who only came from the higher social categories—and it involved a lot of paperwork. That was true of all the world's major economies.

Since then one of Britain's biggest banks, Barclays, has reduced the number of its branches by one-third. Its great rival

National Westminster is in the process of reducing its staff by another 10,000. Even the rock-solid Swiss are having to reduce the number of their bankers. The merger of Swiss Bank Corporation and Union Bank of Switzerland announced in December 1997 could lead to the loss of 3,000 jobs at the two giant institutions, almost half their combined staff. Moreover, those who remain employed in banking are doing radically different jobs from their predecessors.

All this change is exhausting, exciting, and frightening, and sometimes it is all of these things at the same time. But if you are hoping that it is a one-off extraordinary change, forget it. For the next few years are sure to be much more tumultuous than anything we have seen so far. At Andersen Consulting we fully expect there to be more change over the next five years than there has been in the past 20.

The forces for change

The pace of change is accelerating so fast because a number of the forces that bring about change are building up simultaneously. These forces come from consumers, from markets, and from suppliers. It is as if several tornadoes were coming together at once. Individually their impact might not be very powerful, but together they are awesome. A number of tornadoes coming together are far more powerful than the sum of their parts because the interplay between them causes extremely rapid shifts in pressure, shifts that are impossible to predict.

In this book I hope to be able to show that this rapid pace of change in the business world today, and our growing awareness of it, are not things to shrink from. None of us can hope to predict the future, but that is no reason for us to be content to grope ahead blindly.

Andy Grove, chief executive of Intel, *Time* magazine's Man

of the Year for 1997 and someone considered to be at the cutting edge of today's business world, has admitted that, 'On any given day, those of us who work in the high-tech industry make decisions that are basically educated guesses about the future of technology and—equally important—about future market trends.'

Sometimes those guesses can be wildly wrong. Bill Gates, the chairman of Microsoft and the richest man in the world, once said that we would never need a computer with more than 640K of memory. Today you need a minimum of 25 times that!

The best that anybody, not just trailblazers in Silicon Valley, can hope to do about our ever-changing future is to make educated guesses. We know that our vision is limited, and our ability to see ahead little better than that of the early twentieth-century mayor in Pennsylvania who—upon first seeing a telephone—said: 'I can foresee the day when there will be one of these in every town'.

To make the best guesses possible about the future we need to have some sort of vision of that future. And any vision that we create has to be based on an understanding of what it is that is bringing about change in our world now. Only then can we sensibly guess where it is that today's forces for change might ultimately lead us.

The Information Age

One of the most powerful influences on business in the last 50 years has been the way in which the gathering and transmission of information has changed. From being a discrete activity that took place at fixed times and places, it has become a continuous process that takes place everywhere, all the time.

It has progressed from the time more than 50 years ago when all over the world people huddled around radios at fixed moments of the day to catch the most reliable information about the first truly global war, to today, when the Internet gives anybody with a PC and a modem access to immeasurable amounts of information from all corners of the earth.

Radio was followed by television whose pictures transmitted information far in excess of that of radio's sound. Satellites then enabled that information to encircle the globe, and it demonstrated its formidable power by helping to undermine and eventually to bring down communism in Russia and eastern Europe.

'Auf die Dauer fällt die Mauer', said the graffiti on the Berlin Wall. 'With time the wall will fall'. The forecast proved cannily correct. But the graffiti writer probably did not foresee how little time it would take, and almost certainly did not foresee the manner of its falling. It required none of the arsenal of the Cold War; only the bits and bytes that were zapped over the Wall to show the increasingly superior quality of life in the West.

Since then the Internet has been born, and its political and social implications have scarcely begun to show through. Like each new information wave that has hit us, it has not replaced earlier waves. Rather, it has simply rolled on top of them while they themselves have grown even bigger. Radio stations multiply like rabbits, and even the printed word that preceded them has defied predictions of a paperless society—the number of morning newspapers in the United States has increased from about 500 at the beginning of the 1980s to almost 700 today.

The influence of IT

Technological developments have shaped the Information Age, and information technology (IT) has shaped the business world today. *The Economist* said recently that, 'Together, globalisation and IT crush time and space'. Notice that they don't just meddle with it; they crush it. What used to take a year to get to market now takes a month. What used to be made in Stuttgart and sold in Munich is now made in Vietnam and sold in Costa Rica. Once upon a time it was said that when Wall Street sneezes, London catches a cold. Nowadays when Bangkok sneezes, Wall Street catches a cold.

Together, globalisation and IT crush time and space.

The Economist

All purchasers of IT equipment are familiar with the dilemma of second-guessing where the industry is going. What should they be buying now when it will almost certainly be obsolete in less than two years' time? One big accounting firm recently decided to depreciate its laptop computers over two years. Before July 1995 they were depreciated over three years; by July 1999 they will probably be depreciated over one year . . . the same time frame as the office paper clips.

On the Internet a 'web-year' is being defined as 35 calendar days, a reflection of the frenzy of on-line innovation. The equivalent of the innovation that takes place in a year in the rest of the world takes place in only 35 days on the Web. The amount of content—or 'stuff'—on the Web doubles every nine months and the average life of a web page has been estimated as 45 days.

After a slow start, electronic commerce (eCommerce) is taking off. Computer manufacturer Dell is selling $1 million-worth of PCs on the Internet every day and is expecting that to rise to an annual $1 billion-worth by the year 2000. The Internet is well on its way to providing an interactive electronic channel to every home and business in the world. That's the big deal about the Internet.

So big are the changes being brought about by electronics that at Andersen Consulting we believe that there is a fundamental shift taking place in developed economies. We are, we believe, in the process of moving from an industrial economy into what we have termed an electronic economy or 'eEconomy'. This eEconomy has its own distinct and unique characteristics that we are only just beginning to understand. I will say more about the eEconomy later.

The changes in IT are having enormous knock-on effects in other industries. *Fortune* magazine says, 'Microsoft wants to deliver video on-line. Think of it as news you can choose, and consider what it will do to the linear world of TV.' Microsoft already has links with businesses that bring it into direct competition with major media groups such as Time Warner and News Corporation. It owns more than 10% of Comcast, one of America's largest cable companies, and it has a joint venture with the Disney corporation to develop material for the Internet.

The aim of these ventures is to deliver whatever video or audio entertainment you (the customer) wants, whenever you want it. Although the quality of reproduction is not yet perfect, there is already a vast quantity of musical entertainment available on the Internet. Pop star George Michael invites aspiring groups all over the world to send their songs to his record label electronically via the Net, and CD-quality music can already be downloaded to customers via the Internet. What sort of future does that foretell for record stores and traditional music distributors?

Microsoft wants to deliver video on-line. Think of it as news you can choose, and consider what it will do to the linear world of TV.

Fortune, July 1996

Fear and uncertainty

In the face of such fast and unpredictable change it is easy to be fatalistic, to believe that all behaviour is random and its outcome pure chance; to feel that markets are so unpredictable that business is inevitably going to be blown willy-nilly between the poles of extreme wealth and extreme poverty, of fantastic profits and the bankruptcy courts.

The people who have to run industry and commerce under such circumstances are, not surprisingly, fearful and confused. Most managers were trained to manage conventional risk with techniques such as planned obsolescence and oligopolistic competition. In practice, they are having to cope in markets where the rules have undergone fundamental and permanent change, where 70% of the computer industry's revenues come from products that did not exist two years ago, and where Intel can forecast that the power of its microprocessors will soon double at no extra cost. In this world, business's traditional products and services must be continually blended into new value propositions.

On top of all this, businesspeople are being told that continuous improvement is not enough for them to survive. They must also be reinventing their products and services all the time. 'Enterprises must achieve continuous innovation if they expect to hold their pricing above commodity levels,' says my colleague Glover Ferguson, director of Andersen's eCommerce programme.

But how long can a business go on accelerating the pace at which it creates new products and services? Is innovation an unlimited resource?

Employees today are also aware of the uncertainty created by more rapid change. They are having to learn how to live in a world where there are no jobs for life any more, where bank managers and civil servants are as directly exposed to market forces as entrepreneurs and actors. It is a painful lesson, and not just for those who have lost their job.

Gone are other old certainties too—certainties about what to buy, where and when, and about what to manufacture, where and when. They have been undermined by our knowledge of the variety of choice and the speed of change. In their place has come uncertainty, confusion and fear.

The proliferation of information is a mixed blessing. Wide public access to knowledge that it is nigh on impossible to avoid has created large new groups of people for whom excuses for remaining in 'blissful' ignorance no longer exist. The good news is that we have unlimited choices; the bad news is . . . that we have unlimited choices.

Imagine sending an electronic search agent to find prices for a particular product, and that agent comes back with 100 different options. All are equally priced and you've heard of none of the companies. How do you choose between them?

In such an environment are we bound to feel that we are the victims of circumstance rather than the masters of our fate?

The answer has to be, 'No, not necessarily'. Business life need not be gloomily predetermined. By following a few simple steps, companies can build sound strategies for moving forward into the swirling fog that is their future. For despite that fog, the future is still as much to be made as it is something that just happens.

Part of the secret lies in the attitude we have when going into a business adventure. If we see the changes that we face as being fun and opportunistic, then they will be. There's an old saying that fate is what life hands you, and destiny is how you choose to respond to it. In today's world, constant change is our fate. How we respond to that change determines the destiny of our corporations, and of ourselves as well.

What is happening

Any process of learning to live with the future has to begin with a better understanding of today. So in this book I first try to analyse the big changes that are taking place in business now. What are they? Where are they coming from, and where can we imagine them leading to?

Chapter 1 identifies one of the biggest changes in recent years as being the collapse of traditional barriers between industries. No longer do bankers stick to banking and car manufacturers to manufacturing cars. In 1987 the world laughed when the brothers Maurice and Charles Saatchi attempted to buy the then ailing Midland Bank with their advertising agency. A mere ten years later, there was scarcely an industry to be found that was not making a foray into financial services.

Gone are the straightforward industrial categories beloved of statisticians. Retailers are becoming bankers. Tesco has a bank, and the Ford Motor Company has a financial services group, Ford Credit makes more profit annually than Royal Bank of Canada. Virgin has spawned an airline and a chain of music stores. Mitsubishi makes cars and air-conditioning units (and owns a bank). And Ferrari 'sells' after-shave.

The walls that used to retain companies within one (or maybe two) main businesses are crumbling (Figure 1). And not necessarily in traditional ways. It is no longer necessary to be an

Figure 1   How many of us believed that the Berlin Wall could fall?

old-style conglomerate along the lines of an ITT or Hanson in order to be in a lot of businesses. New types of alliances between organisations are being developed all the time—alliances that do not demand that a company own and control all the assets from which it benefits. For example, IBM has set up more than 800 alliances with other companies during the 1990s.

Alliances are a particularly useful way for companies to put an exploratory toe into new industrial waters. The British satellite broadcaster BSkyB has formed a joint venture with British Telecom, Midland Bank and Matsushita Electric (a more unlikely bunch of partners would, five years ago, have been hard to imagine) to go into the high-risk new business of interactive television. I have already mentioned Disney's venture with Microsoft. But Disney also has a host of other alliances with the likes of the German media giant Bertelsmann and the Hearst Corporation. These novel ways of working with traditional rivals in non-traditional businesses have profound implications for all chief executives.

Every manager has to keep asking himself, again and again, 'What business should my company be in?' 'Who are my competitors?' 'Who will they be tomorrow?' For the choices for business leaders today are wider than they have ever been.

Why these changes are occurring

In Chapter 2 I consider why the walls between industries are breaking down, and why they are breaking down now. I start by looking at a number of the major drivers of change in business today—and I divide these into those drivers that can be said to be 'pulling' change along, and those that can be said to be 'pushing' it along.

Consumers, for example, are pulling change with their needs and their demands—and especially with their demand for convenience. Markets and suppliers, on the other hand, are pushing change because they know that they have to be ahead of their rivals all the time, to innovate continuously just to survive.

Consumer behaviour has undergone big changes in recent years. Consumers are, for example, travelling like never before, and bringing home with them new tastes. They are also watching television much more and being made more rapidly aware of what is new on the market.

As they have gained more choice, consumers have also become more discerning and more demanding. Gone are the days when they took whatever was on offer, or waited for it for an indefinite period. Consumers today know what they want, and they want it now.

This puts suppliers in a double bind. Not only are they having to compete with more (and more determined) rivals, but they are also having to cope with more demanding customers. Consumer power is putting pressure on suppliers to serve their customers better. In many cases that means giving them more for less. USAA, an American insurance company, does not just give its customers a cheque to replace their broken vase; it gives them the option of a new vase.

Other changes in consumer behaviour have also had a big impact. Concern for the environment, for example, and the rise of individualism in many countries. But the demand for convenience has probably had the greatest effect of all. Consumers now want goods and services at times and in places that suit them, not the supplier. At the most obvious level this has forced shops and supermarkets to alter their opening hours. These days very few businesses can stay competitive and be open only from 9 a.m. to 5 p.m.

Much change in demand has arisen from changing demographics. In the western world populations are ageing. Not only do the over-60s represent a larger percentage than ever before (and an increasingly more powerful political voice, especially in the United States), but they also represent an increasingly attractive market. Several non-life insurance companies only take customers over the age of 50. The risk of their being involved in an automobile accident or of burning their house down is considerably less than that of younger generations. One of America's most successful small banks, the Bank of Granite in Granite Falls, North Carolina, takes most of its deposits from the elderly. They are, says the bank's chairman John Forlines, 'the ones with all the money'.

Other demographic shifts have had a big effect on business: the rapid urbanisation of many developing countries, for instance, the rise in single-parent families, and the growing number of working women and of family units where both parents are working. In the United States, not only are there more working wives than there were 20 years ago, those wives are also working far longer hours than they did 20 years ago.

In trend-setting California their needs are being met by 'dial-a-wife' services which take on many of the domestic tasks that were carried out by housewives before they became major breadwinners. 'Domestic outsourcers' not only do obvious tasks like plan a menu, cook a meal, collect the kids and arrange household repairs, they can also hunt for missing shirts and recommend the best wholemeal bread in the neighbourhood.

Perhaps the most profound demographic change, though, is the fact that there will be 800 million teenagers in the world in 2001. These 'global' teenagers will reside mostly in non-western nations.

The list of the forces that have been pushing industry to change has to start with technology. Much of this is information technology, the ways of shuffling and disseminating electronic data that are the basis of our Information Age. But other technologies are important too. And in particular military technology. It is remarkable how many of the most promising commercial inventions of recent years have emerged from military research and development.

The technology behind on-board guidance systems in cars is partly based on the military use of satellites to pinpoint any location on earth. Added to sensors in a car's wheels which pick up its direction and the distance travelled, together with a CD-ROM containing a map of the region where the car is travelling, it is possible to create in-car guidance systems that direct the driver to any address anywhere.

The Internet itself arose from the military's need for a communications network that would be able to resist a nuclear strike. It was then taken up by the academic world, where it remained the exclusive province of 'boffins' until its market potential was opened up with the development of user-friendly interfaces.

The effect of these rapid developments in technology on business are deep-seated. Companies today know that if they wait to respond to others in their market they are losing. They have to be leading from the front, inventing new products and services all the time. Many companies aspire to match the much admired American group 3M which sets a target each year for the percentage of its sales that must come from products that did not exist five years ago. That target rises remorselessly every year.

Technological changes are helping industry to find new ways to add value to products and services that have been turned into commodities. When selling commodities there are only two methods of competing: one is on price, and the other is on value. Technology is enabling more and more firms to take this second option. Supermarkets, for example, are starting to sell 'meals' instead of just selling baked beans.

For many industries their markets have become so overcrowded that companies are forced to look for new ways to make money. Drug manufacturers, for example, who find that their margins are continually diminishing, look to make inroads into new fast-growing businesses such as health care. Instead of funding massive R&D efforts to invent new pills, it has become easier for them to stay close to the biotech market and to buy start-ups with promising products.

Another significant force for change has been the widening appreciation of the value that consumers place on brands. Companies have realised not only that consumers will pay a premium for a brand that they trust, but also that the consumers' trust can be stretched to unrelated products and services that carry the same brand name. Thus Virgin's name is written on aeroplanes, trains and on cola cans. And Harley Davidson sells a line of outdoor leisurewear as well as motorbikes.

Manufacturers have also become aware that getting products to market in as short a time as possible is increasingly vital. *Tomorrow's World*, a long-running UK television programme that shows new industrial research and product development, used to seem very futuristic. Viewers could be sure that the gadgets and ideas demonstrated would not appear in shops for a good long while. Today, however, the things the programme shows are often for sale in a matter of months.

The same phenomenon affects authors. I was tempted to make this an electronic product so that I could update it continually. As the production process continued I frequently had to rewrite sections as new developments overtook us. What was a 'will be' rapidly became an 'is'.

Predicting the unpredictable

In Chapter 3 I ask where all this is heading? An old Arab proverb has it that, 'He who predicts the future lies, even if he tells the truth.' Which is wise and true, for we cannot say what the future holds; it will indeed always be uncertain. Still, we can have a vision of where we think things are going. Without a vision we cannot hope to determine in which direction we should be facing.

It may turn out that we are in much the same position as the tourist who asked the Irishman the way to Limerick: 'If that's where you're going,' said the Irishman, 'then I wouldn't be starting from here.' Chapter 3 helps us to determine the place that we should be starting from.

The traditional way of looking into the future has been to extrapolate from the past. But if that were infallible half the world today would be messengers. That they are not is due to Alexander Graham Bell and the invention of the telephone.

Extrapolating from the past has led planners along many false trails. Setting American defence strategy based on experience of the previous decades worked well for a while, but only until the fall of communism. Nuclear warheads and million-man armies don't work well in a world of terrorist groups and fundamentalism. US defence strategy was hit by what Professor Michael Porter of the Harvard Business School has called a 10X force.

A 10X force is something quite out of the ordinary, a force beyond tornado intensity that brings about extraordinary change. The invention of the computer was a 10X force that uprooted forecasts that by the end of this century half of all female workers would be typists and half of all males would be accountants.

A 10X force can on occasions hit an individual firm. One hit the Finnish company Nokia to transform it from a national paper business into a leading European manufacturer of mobile telephones in less than 20 years. Another caused the 111-year-old electrical company Westinghouse to be dissolved at the end of 1997 in order to be resurrected as CBS Corporation, a media group that owns one of America's leading television networks.

Scenario planning

This book's way of looking into the future breaks free from extrapolation and its shortcomings and turns to a technique called scenario planning. Developed by Herman Kahn in the 1960s and by the late Pierre Wack and his team at Royal Dutch/Shell in the 1970s, scenario planning is credited with helping Shell to brace itself for the OPEC-induced oil price hike of 1974. At the time Shell was uniquely able to differentiate itself from almost all the other oil majors.

> *Scenario planning is credited with helping Shell to brace itself for the OPEC-induced oil price hike of 1974.*

One of Pierre Wack's colleagues at Shell was an American called Peter Schwartz. Schwartz is now president of an organisation called Global Business Network (GBN) based in California, near San Francisco, and is currently one of the world's foremost exponents of scenario planning.

In his book, *The Art of the Long View*, published by Doubleday in 1991, Schwartz described in simple terms the foundations of scenario planning.

'Scenarios are a tool for helping us to take a long view in a world of great uncertainty... Scenarios are stories about the way the world might turn out tomorrow, stories that can help us recognise and adapt to changing aspects of our present environment. They form a method for articulating the different pathways that might exist for you tomorrow, and finding your appropriate movements down each of those possible paths. Scenario planning is about making choices today with an understanding of how they might turn out.'

Scenario planning is now being used by strategic planners in corporations and governments across Europe, America and the

Far East. Even the US Department of Defense uses it. On one occasion a few years ago it invited GBN to prepare some scenarios on national security. One of them was called 'Hyperturbulence', and it painted a picture of a world in which the Pentagon was almost totally preoccupied with internal defence issues such as homegrown terrorism.

At a time when Muslim fanatics were striking fear into the heart of governments across the globe, and when Russia seemed to be disintegrating into chaos as it made the painful shift to capitalism, internal terrorism in the United States sounded like nothing more than interesting fiction. But then out of the blue came the bombing in Oklahoma City, and the Defense Department rushed to review the Hyperturbulence scenario in order to have a framework in which to think about what the United States might expect next.

Scenarios allow us to dream for a while, not of the totally fantastic but of the possible and the probable, and of what they might mean for our lives in the future. As some commentators have pointed out, the end of the Millennium has in a way foreshortened our perspective of the future. The film *2001: A Space Odyssey* came out in 1968, and we have not looked much beyond 2001 since. I believe it is time for all of us to stretch our horizons a good bit further into the next century.

The business community in particular needs to look further ahead. Its nervous concern with the Year 2000 problem (the fact that many computers are programmed to identify years by their last two digits and so cannot tell the difference between 1 January 1901 and 1 January 2001) has lulled business into thinking that once it has surmounted that particular hurdle it will move into the Elysian fields of the twenty-first century. But the beginning of the twenty-first century will be little different from the end of the twentieth. The difference will only be in people's minds; on the ground, problems will intensify and persist.

Chapter 3 looks at ways in which scenario planning can help businessmen and women to make choices in the difficult years ahead. It focuses on assessing the risks and rewards that attach to the various possible outcomes that follow from choices. 'It is,' says Schwartz, 'the ability to act with a knowledgeable sense of risk and reward that separates both the business executive and the wise individual from a bureaucrat or a gambler.'

The stories unfold

In the five chapters that follow—the meat of the book—I tell five different stories. They are not the only stories I could have told, but I had to limit the book somehow. Each of the five I have chosen represents a different view of the future, and each one tries to make that view more real by putting flesh and bones onto an outline of how business might develop over the next ten years.

None of the five stories is going to happen in exactly the way I suggest, but elements from all of them are sure to appear widely over the next ten years.

The stories are based on our identification of two major engines of change in the business world today: the pull that comes from increasingly demanding consumers; and the push that comes from the fear of suppliers that they will be left behind if they are not being innovative every moment of their corporate lives. These two drivers we can plot as two separate axes at right angles to each other (Figure 2 opposite).

The axes thus represent different outcomes for:

1 **The consumer.** Will consumers want to choose from a multitude of predefined products that have, as is largely the case today, been ready-made for them? Or will they seek more and more to co-design and/or co-produce products to meet their needs? That is to say, will they want to make price-based

purchasing decisions on commodities (be they savings accounts or baked beans), or will they want to make value-based purchasing decisions that provide solutions (how to get the children to school, for instance, or what meal to serve their guests tonight). At one end of this axis lies what I have called the 'buyer' and at the other lies the 'co-producer', the customer who wants to be involved in finding solutions to his or her everyday problems.

2 **The supplier.** In the future, will companies operate throughout the entire value chain; the chain of processes that convert raw materials into finished products and services? Or will they prefer to be specialists concentrating on one particular aspect of that chain? Can we expect companies in the future to be categorised by the things that they produce (as manufacturers of automobiles or of soap powder, for example) or by where they operate in the chain (as packagers of all sorts of things or as designers of internal combustion engines)? At

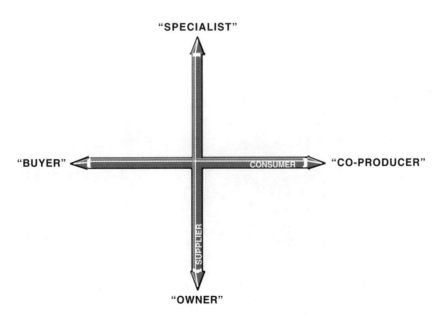

Figure 2   The two major engines of change

one end of this axis lies the 'specialist' and at the other lies the 'owner', i.e. the supplier who wants to own and control all the processes involved in bringing a product to market.

Taking these two axes so that they dissect each other creates, as it were, four panes of a window. The extreme outside corners of these four panes represent the first four of our five scenarios (Figure 3).

The chapters about these scenarios follow a similar format. Beginning with a description of the business world in the year 2008, they go on to analyse the scenario from the point of view of the consumer, the marketplace and the supplier. They then describe in more detail what some of the major companies of the day—Ford, Nokia, etc.—will be doing under the scenario. At the same time they suggest what companies will have to do to be successful in such circumstances. And finally they look at what sort of early warning signs there will be to indicate that the world is going in that particular direction.

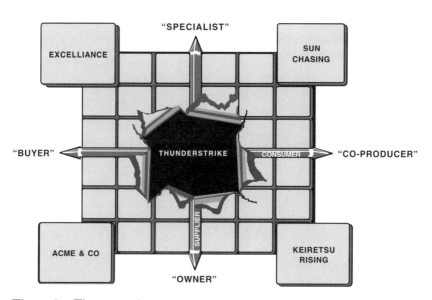

Figure 3   Five scenarios

1   In the top right-hand pane of our window is the specialist/co-producer scenario. This I have called **Sun Chasing**. In this vision of the future, consumers are in control and they invite global companies to satisfy their individual needs. Technology and globalisation have led to a revolutionary change in what consumers buy and how it is delivered to them. At the same time, new ways of working have created an exploding economy. Global unemployment is at an all-time low.

2   In the bottom right-hand pane of the window is the owner/co-producer scenario which I have called **Keiretsu Rising**. Keiretsu is a Japanese word meaning, literally, 'headless combine'. It is the name given to the widely admired form of Japanese corporate structure in which a number of independently managed companies own small stakes in each other and work together in a variety of ways. It is increasingly being mirrored in the west in the networks of alliances that companies (such as IBM and Disney) are forming with each other.

In our Keiretsu Rising scenario the world is populated by vast diversified conglomerates which try to 'own' customers and satisfy a broad range of their needs. (The larger Japanese keiretsu already supply a range of goods and services that can stretch all the way from banking to air-conditioning.) While the outputs of these conglomerates in future will change, based on consumer demand, their sheer size will allow them to cater to consumer needs without having to reach outside the resources of their own cartel. Many of them will be of such a size and scope that they would not have held up to the scrutiny of anti-trust authorities a decade earlier.

3   Our third scenario combines the supplier as owner and the customer as buyer, and lies in the bottom left-hand corner of the window made by our axes. I have called it **Acme & Co**, and it is characterised by extremely large, vertically integrated companies that are competing fiercely for local market share while at the same time investing in developing markets elsewhere. Price is the key influence on customers and there is little differentiation of products. The companies that succeed are masters of re-engineering and cost reduction, and they can decide to stop newcomers in their tracks. Through mergers and acquisitions, the world's leading corporations become so large, and they do so much that cuts across traditional industry boundaries, that most business classifications are reorganised by company rather than by industry.

4   The last of the scenarios formed by the intersecting axes of consumers' and suppliers' future behaviour lies in the top left-hand corner, the pane that combines the 'specialist' supplier with the 'buyer' consumer. In this scenario, which I have termed **Excelliance**, a combination of Excellence and Alliance, the level of excellence needed to succeed on an increasingly global playing field makes it difficult for companies to be much more than one thing to any one customer. Alliances of global process specialists come together to offer standardised products in crowded price-driven markets. Companies come to excel at their core skills and to outsource non-core skills (usually to alliance partners). Organisations are no longer known for creating a particular type of product; instead they are recognised for being excellent at a particular type of process.

5   Our fifth scenario is a wildcard that falls quite outside the axes that shape the other four. Called **Thunderstrike**, it arises from imagining a complete disaster, a situation in which companies work to survive throughout an extended period of conflict. The world economy is in chaos; war is spreading throughout Asia; and an ultra-nationalist government has just reclaimed Russia. The world is strafed by war, poverty and

fear, and 'consumers' have all but disappeared. In their place are people who look more like 'survivors'.

What can we do?

Having taken a peek into the future in this way, we all naturally want to know what we can do to increase our chances of success in this future. So in Chapter 9 I make some suggestions that are designed to help businesses hedge their bets on the twenty-first century.

In general, I have three main recommendations:

✦ First, that companies should follow robust strategies, i.e. do those things that hold good more or less regardless of which scenario unfolds. (And despite the threat of accelerating change, there are still a few things that do fall into that category!)
✦ Second, businesses should monitor early warning signs in order to help them identify at the earliest possible opportunity which scenario is beginning to predominate. The failure of business alliances to fulfil their promise, for example, may suggest that the nature of supply is less likely to be collaborative. It does not, however, say anything about demand or consumer behaviour.
✦ Finally, corporate leaders should engage their management team in thinking openly about the future. For regardless of which scenario unfolds, success will depend on groups of individuals working together in ad hoc teams that are able to react to change both quickly and flexibly. This may sound like apple pie, but it is remarkable to me how few organisations do think freely about the future.

In order to help you further, I have included at the end of the book some details of a game that we have devised around our scenarios. Called Destination Z, it takes teams of executives on a journey in which they are compelled to think in a structured way about the future of their organisation. Not only has almost everybody who has participated in the game found it enormously helpful, they have also found it to be enormous fun, as should be the real journey that takes organisations into that great unknown—the future.

1

The Walls Come Tumbling Down

BEFORE WE POLISH OUR CRYSTAL BALLS AND TAKE A LOOK into the future we need to have a sound understanding of the present. What are the things that are happening now that are going to be the most powerful influences in shaping that future?

I believe that the most significant change taking place today is the dismantling of the walls that have traditionally separated businesses from each other. There was a time when car companies made cars and banks sold financial services, and each did little else. When the Saatchi brothers attempted to take over Midland Bank in 1987, they were one of the first to suggest that running a bank might be much like running any other service industry. At the time, bank regulators were horrified at the idea, and the deal failed to get the go-ahead. But since then the business world has changed to such an extent that car companies do now sell financial services, and none of us thinks it strange.

Companies such as Virgin have proved that it is possible to embrace almost any line of business. There is Virgin Cola, and there is the very visible Virgin airline. There are Virgin financial products, Virgin records, Virgin cinemas, and more. One of the few where the assets are owned and run by the Virgin organisation in a traditional way is the airline. For many, Virgin is just a marketing and sales organisation that fronts a business run by others.

More and more industries are following this path, seeing the Virgin structure as a model for the future. Every company now has the opportunity to go into any business that it fancies. The graffiti on the Berlin Wall today applies to every industry: 'Auf die Dauer Fällt die Mauer', 'With time the wall will fall' (Figure 4). The wall between your industry and any other that you care to name may collapse tomorrow, with unforeseeable implications.

What, for instance, will be the implications for the water industry now that power companies have decided that running one utility is much like running another? Which utility 'brand' is going to come to the fore? And how long will it be before we have Virgin Water and Virgin Power?

Behind the fall of industry's walls lie a number of more detailed trends among firms that I see as being particularly significant. In the rest of this chapter I look at my 'Top Ten', the

Figure 4   'With time the wall will fall'—graffiti on the Berlin Wall

ten shifts currently taking place in corporate behaviour that I believe provide the most telling pointers to the future.

These 'top ten' shifts are:

1 The broadening of the range of products and services on offer.
2 The creation of new value propositions.
3 The virtualisation of organisations.
4 The way that companies are getting closer to their customers.
5 The addition of demergers to traditional mergers and acquisitions (M&A).
6 The formation of strategic alliances.
7 The growth of outsourcing.
8 Expanding globalisation.
9 The rapid entry of newcomers into old markets.
10 Customisation.

Broadening the range

Virgin is an extreme example of the many companies that are broadening the range of products and services that they offer to customers. Some of the best examples come from retailing. In the UK, for instance, supermarkets have become major retailers of petrol; a domain previously reserved for the retail operations of the major oil refiners. UK supermarkets now account for almost one-quarter of all UK petrol sales (up from 5% a decade ago).

In response to this competition for their traditional business, the petrol retailers are moving in the opposite direction and starting to expand their forecourts. Often situated in prime sites, they are being developed in order to sell a range of food and other products that are also sold in supermarkets. In Scandinavia, the trend has gone so far that Texaco has opened a petrol-less petrol station at which it sells only non-petrol items.

At the same time supermarkets are expanding beyond the petrol forecourt and threatening to provide some of the biggest challenges for financial institutions. 'Supermarkets are queuing up to be superbanks', said one UK newspaper headline in late 1997. Safeway in the UK has launched an in-house debit card and a 24-hour telephone banking service, and Sainsbury and Tesco have linked up with the Bank of Scotland and the Royal Bank of Scotland, respectively to offer banking services under their own brands—Sainsbury's Bank and Tesco Personal Finance. Services are operated primarily over the telephone, not inside the stores.

The supermarkets are not motivated primarily by a desire to improve their margins. After all, the banking business is also very crowded at its commodity end, which is where the supermarkets are offering services. Rather, they are making this move as a way to protect their customer base. The loss of 10% of a supermarket's customers can be disastrous. What better way to cement relationships with them than to provide their banking services as well?

The success of the supermarkets' ventures into banking is not yet assured. Most go along with the Royal Bank of Scotland's chief executive George Mathewson who has been quoted as saying: 'I'm reluctant to bet the business on any one distribution channel'. Threatening to revolutionise the supermarket business—and indeed the banking business—is eCommerce and the growing use of the Internet as a distribution channel for both banking and shopping.

Britain's banks have not taken the competition from the retailers lightly. In 1996 two senior executives (from Marks & Spencer and Tesco) left the board of Lloyds TSB, Britain's biggest bank, because of the growing competition that they then saw between their business and the banks'.

In the USA it is difficult for supermarkets to get into financial services because of the high wall that the Glass-Steagall

Act puts around the banking industry. But that is not stopping banks moving into supermarkets. In California, Wells Fargo bank now has about as many of its branches inside supermarkets as it has outside them. And in some of its branches it is taking on the supermarkets at their own game and selling pharmaceutical products. A bank that sells toothpaste! Whatever next?

The Glass-Steagall's walls are looking increasingly vulnerable these days, and one person who is watching for their fall is Microsoft's chairman Bill Gates. He was widely reported when he said:

> *Banks are dinosaurs. Give me a piece of the transaction business and they're history.*
>
> *Bill Gates*

Microsoft's ambitions to broaden its range of products and services are not restricted to financial services. It already has an alliance with American Express whose goal, say the two firms without undue modesty, is to 'reinvent the travel process'. And I have already mentioned Microsoft's involvement in joint ventures with America's media giants—a 50/50 joint venture with broadcaster NBC, for example, which is looking to narrow the gap between the television and the computer. (NBC is owned by General Electric, which is itself a large producer of television sets.)

In Germany, non-banks are allowed to sell a wide range of financial services, and car manufacturer Volkswagen owns a bank and is one of the largest non-bank providers of financial services in Europe. It is now using its experience in providing customers with car loans to stretch its financial services business still further—into mortgages and savings instruments.

There is some debate about the dangers of broadening an organisation's range of products in this way. Some fear that brands become devalued by being associated with almost anything. But others say there is no limit to how far they can be stretched. Virgin could front a fast-food franchise as well as a waste management business.

For sure, whenever a first-class brand such as Virgin is attached to a new product or service, customers' expectations are aroused. When Virgin took over the running of the UK's west coast railways, for example, long-suffering passengers expected dramatic improvements overnight. When they failed to appear, Virgin felt obliged to make announcements saying that they were working on making things better, but that it would take time for improvements to show through.

Richard Branson's answer to those who think he may have pushed the Virgin brand too far is unambiguous. 'Each time Virgin entered a new business all the conventional pundits whined that we were stretching our brand too far', he says. 'Rather than worrying too much about brands being stretched too far, people will have to stretch their imaginations further.'

Creating new value propositions

As companies are presented with an ever-wider range of business opportunities, they are indeed having to stretch their imaginations further. They are constantly being challenged to come up with innovative new ways of creating value.

The chairman of Revlon once gathered his sales force together and asked them what business they were in. They all assumed that it was an easy question and replied without too much thought, 'The business of selling cosmetics.' 'No', said the chairman soberly. 'You are in the business of selling dreams.' Now when you are in the business of selling dreams, you can sell a lot more than cosmetics.

Likewise Formula One motor racing is selling a lot more than cars driving around a racetrack. It is selling excitement, and when you're selling excitement you have a lot of options for new business. Ferrari, for example, has launched an after-shave that is proving very popular.

The controversy over tobacco sponsorship of Formula One racing is partly based on this. Audiences do not just see Marlboro's name on a fast car and think, 'Cigarettes'. They see Marlboro's name on a fast car and think, 'Excitement'. And then they think 'Cigarettes'.

An example of how to add value comes from the mortgage business. Supplying mortgages today in sophisticated western financial markets is a commodity business. A supplier in the UK will be competing with about 150 other institutions to sell a service where the purchasing decision is nearly always made on price.

However, a supplier who looks at the customer from a slightly different angle sees a different business. He sees someone who is not just looking for a mortgage, but who is in fact wanting to buy a house. Now buying a house means moving home, and moving home is the third most stressful thing that happens to individuals in wealthy nations at the end of the twentieth century (after divorce and the death of a loved one).

With this in mind I carried out some research to see which part of the house-buying process caused the most aggravation. I broke up the process of moving house into its constituent parts and asked members of the public to put them in descending order according to the degree of aggravation that they caused. Near the top of the list came things like:

✦ finding a house to buy;
✦ selling the one you already possess;
✦ moving your possessions out of the house that you are leaving.

Getting a mortgage came way down the list. So a mortgage lender that wants to add value may decide that as a company it should be trying to tackle some higher priority items, or indeed offering to support the whole home-moving process.

Technology is a great help to companies in creating new business propositions and in finding ways to add value. Consider, as an example, the story of a research scientist at Andersen Consulting's Centre for Strategic Technology Research (CSTaR) who recently got married and bought a house in the suburbs of Chicago.

Every few weeks at the scientist's new home the doorbell would ring and a man would be standing on the doorstep with a 50 lb block of salt which he said was for the scientist's water softener. The delivery did not occur at regular intervals. But every time that it did occur, sure enough the water softener needed refreshing.

Baffled by the man's impeccable timing the scientist eventually asked him how he knew so accurately when to come, and it was then explained to him that the water softener was 'smart'. When it detected that it was running out of salt it sent a message to the local service depot and asked to be fed. That meant that the depot got the scientist's custom rather than some random supplier that he might have stumbled across when he eventually realised that he had run out of salt.

In a similarly 'smart' way, major car manufacturers are installing systems that call for emergency assistance and repair whenever there is a collision—another way of combining products and services to create new value propositions.

The embedding of this sort of intelligence into products will undoubtedly increase. There are already vacuum cleaners that automatically adjust to the thickness of the carpet that they are working on. And the intelligent car of the future will be able to warn its service agent that in two (or three, or four) hours time it is going to have a problem with a particular part. There are already aeroplanes with systems that call up a mechanic (and not the pilot) when there is a minor technical problem on board.

Another prospect for adding value in the future is the intelligent rubbish bin! This will be able to read the bar codes of discarded packaging and advise an on-line supplier that the customer requires a replacement. That need not involve sending round a deliveryman every time a carton of milk is thrown away. Rather, the information can be kept on a computer file to become the basis for a weekly list of replacement shopping.

To create new value propositions like this, organisations frequently need to take a step back and ask themselves what businesses they ought to be in. United Services Automobile Association (USAA) is one company that went through such a process and then changed its value proposition as a result. USAA, which began life as an insurance company, has come to use information about its customers in a way that satisfies needs well outside the traditional area of financial services.

The company started by asking how it could differentiate itself from its competitors. And while considering this question it came to realise that for many of its customers the most difficult part of coping with stolen or damaged goods is the actual business of replacing them. It was a problem that had received little or no attention from traditional insurers.

So USAA began to offer its customers a rather different service. Instead of giving them money to replace the vase that had been broken or the car that had been stolen, it actually gave them the option of a new vase or a new car. At the same time it set up a network of retailers whose products it agreed to offer as replacement goods, and for that service it received a commission from the retailers.

To its customers, USAA is not now in the business of insurance. It would be more accurate to say that it is in the business of Winding Back the Clock, of restoring the situation as closely as possible to what it was before the accident happened.

Shifting a company's focus onto new value propositions in this way can gradually change a company altogether. Nokia, for example, was a paper-maker a couple of decades ago. Now it is one of Europe's leading mobile phone companies. Japanese car-maker Toyota has developed an interest in satellite broadcasting. Maybe in 20 years time it will be the world's biggest satellite broadcaster, and it may then again find itself competing fiercely with one of its big rivals of today, General Motors. The American car-maker also has an interest in satellite broadcasting.

Andersen Consulting has itself shifted its focus over the years. It emerged, first of all, from a firm of accountants, and it used to say that it was in the business of solving problems. Then it slightly changed its line and said that it was in the business of 'building business systems'.

Afterwards it moved into the 'management-of-change' business, which was before it got into the business that it is in now—namely, 'the client success business'. As we continue to help our clients change to be more successful, you can be sure that we will continue to change as well (indeed, as I write this book I am aware that we are about to redefine our role again).

Virtualisation

As organisations enter more and more new industries they are creating new structures that are better suited to their new character. Virgin is seen as a pioneer in the creation of the 'virtual organisation'. Virtually nothing in terms of the number of its employees, it is virtually anything in terms of the businesses that it is capable of embracing. The company manages to have its fingers in so many business pies because it does not carry most of the assets that have traditionally been considered essential for those businesses.

I define 'virtualisation' as 'the removal of constraints of time, place and form . . . made possible by the convergence of computing, telecommunications and visual media'. And this is what is happening to financial services and a number of other industries. The constraints of time (branch opening hours), place (branch offices) and form (paper-based applications) are rapidly being removed by IT.

Virtualisation is leaving traditional financial institutions trailing behind nimble newcomers and taking companies into territory that has never been explored before. Virtualise a business and you revolutionise an industry.

In 1995 Virgin Cola captured about 5% of the UK cola market with just five employees. This was achieved by an extraordinarily tight focus on the company's core competence— which was not the manufacturing of cola but the marketing of it. Everything other than marketing, including production of the drink itself, was done by somebody else. The experience of Virgin and others has led me to expound Baldock's law:

A virtual enterprise has 1% of market share per employee

Baldock's Law

Technological and regulatory forces have brought many markets to the point where virtual organisations are the ones best designed to thrive. Virtual organisations can be found in many industries. Aprilia, an Italian motorcycle manufacturer, is another example. Despite having its name on one of the most desired bikes in the world, Aprilia itself does not actually make a single component of the bike.

Business Week describes Aprilia's offices as looking 'more like a California software house than a motorbike manufacturer'. Everything is bought from a network of suppliers spread across northern Italy. Indeed, this system of having a network of small family firms supplying a few big manufacturers is common in Italy (other well-known examples include Benetton and Gucci). It is held up by some as a model for the industrial structure of the future.

Another type of virtual organisation is that run by Bayerische Vereinsbank in Germany. Faced with a dwindling ability to attract younger customers, the old-established Bavarian bank decided to set up a separate operation that would deliver a wider range of banking services exclusively through electronic channels. Called Advance Bank, it is accessible by telephone, fax and the Internet 24 hours a day, seven days a week. The bank's customers do all their banking remotely; and there are no physical assets at all—not even a place where they can queue!

A key feature of virtual organisations is that they can change shape very rapidly. When Virgin first went into financial services in early 1995 it chose as its partner the Norwich Union Life Insurance company. The company was the sixth biggest composite insurer (life and general) in the UK and a pillar of the financial establishment.

However, in November 1995 Virgin decided to switch partners (less than a year after its venture into financial services was first launched). The Norwich Union was swapped in favour of the AMP Society (AMP), a company that Virgin hoped would give it greater global reach.

Virgin was able to switch partners so early in the life of the venture because its customers are hardly ever aware that they are buying anything other than a 100% Virgin product or service. The transition from the Norwich Union to the Australian Mutual was seamless to Virgin's customers. Many of them, who like to see themselves as anti-establishment, might have been surprised had they realised that the actual provider of their services was itself far from being anti-establishment.

Getting closer to the customer

One influence on the way that companies are restructuring themselves is their strong desire to get closer to their customers at a time when their customers are getting more remote through the use of remote channels such as Internet banking. The customer is king like never before, and fickle too like never before. Firms need to keep a close eye on their customers and, wherever possible, anticipate changes in their behaviour if they are to keep them on their side.

Firms have been doing this in two ways: one, by getting to know more about their customers, and two, by cutting out middlemen wherever possible. Middlemen, by definition, act as a barrier between suppliers and their ultimate customer.

Technology has again come to their assistance. In particular, the technology of the telephone and the computer has created new ways for firms to get closer to their customers. Techniques such as data mining, for example, enable people at all levels of an organisation to access more information about their customers more immediately.

The growth of the 'direct' selling of goods and services by telephone is an indication of the extent to which middlemen have been squeezed out of business in recent years. For direct selling means nothing more than that the supplier of goods and services gets into 'direct' contact with the customer.

In the UK, a company called Direct Line was the pioneer in providing telephone-based insurance services, and so successful was it that it forced most major insurers to follow its example. Almost all of them now offer their own 'direct' services. By cutting out the middleman the insurance companies have managed to nearly halve their expense ratios.

Direct Line was founded by Peter Woods who was previously the IT director of a large insurance company. His first big idea was to sell insurance directly to customers over the phone. But he had a second big idea as well, and it was the combination of the two that turned the industry upside down.

His second big idea was to limit the range of customers that Direct Line served, confining it to selling only car insurance to low-risk drivers. Traditional insurance companies charged a 'blended' rate that took account of low-risk and high-risk drivers and which meant that careful drivers subsidised those more prone to accidents. There is no such blending at Direct Line.

Another indication of the desire of firms to get closer to their customers is the growth in 'loyalty' programmes. These are a way for companies to keep in touch with existing customers by rewarding consumers with points for using one supplier rather than another. The points win prizes and help to bind customers to a single supplier.

A number of companies have taken the idea one step further. Safeway, for example, has joined with Shell and others (Ford, Cellnet and Allied Domecq) to develop a joint customer loyalty programme. Joint programmes have the potential to multiply the benefit many times over. In theory, consumers get locked into all the members of the programme as they aim to reap the common benefits.

The squeezing out of middlemen is evident in many places. In stockbroking, for instance, where brokers are intermediaries between investors and the stock market, customers have decided that they don't want to pay for expensive brokers' advice when they don't need it. Investors are more sophisticated than they used to be and the stock market is no longer a frightening mystery. Moreover, they have direct access elsewhere to more and more up-to-date market information.

In America and Europe investors are increasingly turning to no-frills 'execution only' firms which do just what they are told, and no more. In the USA, Schwab's name has become almost synonymous with the low-cost transactional end of the business.

Sharelink, a UK company that offers 'execution only' equity trading by phone, claims that over 40% of the volume of trading on the London Stock Exchange is now carried out by such firms. They are cutting deeply into the business of traditional 'advisory' brokers.

This process can only be accelerated as stockbroking moves from the phone to the PC. There are already firms that enable customers to execute on-line deals via a PC and a modem. Schwab offers an Internet-based service where its strong brand name helps Internet customers overcome their fear about security.

The Internet provides a ubiquitous electronic channel to everybody's doorstep, cutting out intermediaries all over the place. It is going to make the stockbroker little more than an electronic gateway to a stock market that the customer accesses almost directly. The broker's role is being reduced to one of providing checks and balances on the deals that pass through its gateway— to make sure, for example, that the deals are permitted by the rules of the relevant regulators.

In industries such as textiles, direct selling has also had a big impact. With the help of multimedia aids like CD-ROMs, garment industry buyers in Europe and America are communicating directly with factories in India and the Far East, in many cases cutting out the need for an agent in those places. Designers in New York can send their latest designs electronically to factories in Asia where they are cut and sewn in quantities determined by orders that have in turn been gathered electronically from around the world and transmitted to the factory via the Internet. The only travel that needs to be done is by the garments themselves.

The implications of all this may be very wide indeed. In 1996 a German trade official blamed the Internet for a decline in

German exports. He explained that it had enabled potential customers to compare the prices of suppliers all around the world and to use that information to press for the most favourable deal.

Electronic commerce (eCommerce, a wide term that refers to the conduct of business using any electronic means) has only just begun to demonstrate how it can make the relationship between consumers and suppliers more direct. In most developed countries a few tens of thousands of customers are doing their banking via the Internet, and there are a number of scattered experiments in on-line shopping. A service originally available in only west London, for example, allows the residents of Ealing to order groceries over the Net and to have them delivered to their front door for a charge of £5—regardless of the size of the order. This service has now been extended to my area and I can confirm that it is wonderful!

However slow the Internet may have been to take off for commercial purposes, nobody doubts that its use is going to explode over the next few years. One survey of medium-sized companies in the UK found that in June 1997 not one of them had the capacity to do business on the Internet. Yet almost half of them had plans that would enable them to take part in eCommerce within the next 12 months.

Andersen Consulting's own research indicates that as many as 15–20% of US households (or up to 20 million homes) would subscribe to a Consumer Direct service within the next decade. Consumer Direct is any service that enables people to buy groceries, and such things as videos and dry cleaning, by using computers, telephones, faxes or other electronic channels that allow them to shop without actually going to a store.

This figure was more than three times our original estimate of the speed at which electronic shopping would take off. Moreover, the survey showed that interest in electronic shopping was spread across all demographic groups. Although young high-income families were the most keen, there was also plenty of enthusiasm among the elderly.

Writing in *Outlook*, Andersen Consulting's own magazine, consultants David H. Friedman, Victor J. Orler and Frederick Schneider suggested that this 'represents a huge challenge for traditional retailers. If a food retailer loses 10% of its volume to Consumer Direct, it could mean as much as a 50% loss in profitability for a typical retailer. Depending on how quickly a market adopts Consumer Direct, this marketplace shift could significantly affect brick and mortar retailers within the next seven to 10 years, and could have an impact on some markets as soon as three to five years.'

In the long run (and remember that the long run is increasingly short), eCommerce is going to impinge on the strategy of virtually every business on the planet. A report produced by a special taskforce set up by President Clinton estimated that sales of goods and services on-line will grow to $7 billion by the year 2000 (from about $1 billion in 1996).

The implications of this for the relationship between customers and suppliers will be profound. For a start, a system in which goods come to the customer rather than the customer to the goods promises to be many times more efficient than our present way of doing things.

On a more basic level, think about the logistical implications for supermarkets. When shopping is based on home delivery of orders taken via the Net, suppliers require warehouses and a lot of small vans. Yet the method of shopping that we have today requires a lot of shops and a few large vans. The considerations to be taken into account when locating a warehouse for the system of the future are very different from those to be taken into account when locating a shop today. At the very least, it might not be wise for supermarkets to build too many new car parks.

Mergers, acquisitions and demergers

Many companies today are continuing to buy their way into new businesses. The value of M&A (mergers and acquisitions) in 1997 was an all-time high. But today's M&A activity is different from that in the past in at least two significant respects.

In the first instance, it involves far fewer contested take-overs. Most of the mergers taking place these days are between consenting partners. And secondly, much of the activity involves the breaking up of old-style conglomerates. Companies such as ITT and Hanson, which bought collections of companies from across a wide range of industries in the 1970s and 1980s, are being broken up.

The logic of these groups was based on ownership and on rigid central control of all of their diverse bits. When the main reason for putting them together collapsed—the belief that their centre's general management skills could be applied with equal effectiveness to any business—so did they. Christopher Collins, Hanson's deputy chairman, has said: 'We demerge for sound business reasons. We are investing in the future.'

The break-up of the old conglomerates has given the M&A business a new initial. Now it is M&A&D—mergers and acquisitions and demergers.

The modern boundary breakers are very different from the old conglomerates like Hanson. They are built on a network of alliances—looser informal links that allow the businesses to shift and change shape in a flexible way that suits the environment in which they are operating. Their centre is focused on a core competency (be it marketing or logistics) which determines the structure of the rest of the organisation.

Today's corporate amalgams require different metaphors from the belligerent descriptions used to describe corporate take-overs in their hey-day. (Remember *Barbarians at the Gate?*) Some analysts have turned to biology in their search for suitable ways to describe current industrial change. James Moore, a Boston-based consultant and author of *The Death of Competition: Leadership & Strategy in the Age of Business Ecosystems*, says that 'business ecosystem' is a more appropriate term these days than 'industry'. Microsoft, he says, is 'an ecosystem that traverses at least four major industries: personal computers; consumer electronics; information and communications.'

Strategic alliances

The strategies that many companies are using to enter new industries are radically different from the traditional ways in which firms expanded. The options in the olden days could be summed up as 'buy' or 'build'. Firms could either buy businesses from someone else (via mergers and acquisitions) or they could build them up themselves from scratch.

Today's growth-minded businesses, however, often prefer a third option: they prefer to 'borrow' a new business by entering into a joint venture or loose alliance with others who have skills relevant to that business, or who have already put a toe into its waters. This reduces their risk by spreading the cost.

Many big firms have already formed hundreds of different alliances that range from preferential arrangements with suppliers to significant joint ventures involving cross-shareholdings. Managing these networks of alliances has become a major strategic issue for these corporations.

The new corporate structures that have been created to accommodate these networks have led in many cases to a very different culture. An article in the July/August 1996 issue of the *Harvard Business Review* entitled 'How Chrysler Created an American Keiretsu' describes the American car manufacturer's radically new relationships with its suppliers. Not only had

Chrysler slashed their number (from 2,500 in 1989 to 1,140 in 1996), but it had also involved them intimately in subsequent product development and in process improvement.

The company's traditionally adversarial relationship with its suppliers had been turned into a co-operative one. The article's author, Jeffrey H. Dyer, said: 'The two sides now strive together to find ways to lower the costs of making cars and to share the savings'. The author concluded that:

> *Chrysler has proved that highly productive partnerships with suppliers not only can flourish in the United States but are the wave of the future.*
>
> *Jeffrey H. Dyer, Harvard Business Review*

Chrysler was heavily influenced by the way in which Japanese manufacturers such as Honda and Mitsubishi relate to their suppliers. But the American company has stopped short of becoming a full Japanese *keiretsu*. A major Japanese company like Toyota, for example, owns stakes of between 20% and 50% in many of its suppliers, and they become heavily dependent on it for their survival. Such shareholdings do not exist in Chrysler's case, and the American company prefers to describe itself as an 'extended enterprise' rather than a *keiretsu*.

An article in *The New Yorker* in October 1997 describes the way in which this structure has been adopted by another industry in the USA. Entitled 'American Keiretsu' the article showed 'how the six most powerful media companies are borrowing the ancient Japanese custom of co-opting the competition'. A spider's web of a chart laid out the links between Rupert Murdoch's News Corporation, Bill Gates's Microsoft, Walt Disney, General Electric (which owns NBC), Time Warner and Tele-Communications Inc (TCI), a lesser known company which owns 10% of Time Warner and has powerful links with all the others. TCI, News

Corporation and General Electric all have a stake in Madison Square Garden, for example, and five of the six have an interest in Primestar, a satellite television company.

The author, Ken Auletta, goes on to explain why these companies are behaving in this novel way. 'These companies join forces', he says, 'for various reasons. They do so to avoid competition. They do so to save money and share risks. They do so, as Microsoft did with Comsat and Murdoch is doing with Primestar, to buy a seat at an adversary's table. They join forces to create a safety net of sorts, because technology is changing so rapidly that no one can be sure which technology or which business will be ascendant.'

Outsourcing

Outsourcing is another powerful force acting on corporate structures today. Companies are being encouraged to hand over to others all sorts of functions that a few years ago would have been considered integral to their main business and inseparable from it.

Two things in particular are driving them to make this move:

1   The desire to shrink back into what they consider to be their core competencies.
2   The need to get a better service in areas (like IT) that are becoming increasingly specialised.

When J. P. Morgan outsourced its information technology to a consortium of suppliers that included Andersen Consulting, it did so because it had decided that it was not in the business of IT. J. P. Morgan is in the business of banking; Andersen Consulting, on the other hand, is in the business of IT. For J. P. Morgan IT is just a tool to help it carry out its main business; for Andersen Consulting IT is a main business.

Outsourcing helps firms to become more nimble, which is vital when their markets are being attacked from all sides. By converting a fixed cost (the cost of running the function when it was done in-house) to a variable cost (the service charge of the firm that takes on that function), companies can shed capacity and take on extra capacity much more easily and cheaply. The outsourcer is left to manage the cost implications of its client's nimbleness.

Expanding globalisation

As barriers between industries have been breaking down, so have the barriers erected by distance. Companies have scoured the globe for new suppliers and they have also scoured it for new markets. The advertisements that you see on the way into town from the airport of almost any capital city in the world have the same roll call of names—Marlboro, Mercedes-Benz, Coca-Cola, British Airways and Citibank. Drive along main roads in remote eastern Turkey and it is not long before you see the familiar yellow and red of the Shell petrol sign. McDonald's has been a huge success in Moscow, and CNN's news service has been a huge success almost everywhere.

Service industries travel particularly well because they are not so capital intensive. If you look at the world's biggest accounting firms, each of them today has offices in over 100 countries. They have been able to build up this network while legally constituted as partnerships and without the benefit of access to major capital markets.

Andersen Consulting itself has offices in 46 countries, ranging from Argentina to Saudi Arabia and from Hungary to South Korea, a bigger network than any other firm of consultants. World-wide courier companies such as UPS and DHL also have networks that truly circle the globe. Financial services have the capacity to travel great distances too. Citibank, for example, has bank branches in 98 countries, and Merrill Lynch sells securities in 45 countries worldwide.

These days firms like Merrill Lynch offer much more to their clients, be they in America or elsewhere, than the shares of a few American blue-chip companies. The 'thundering herd' is busily selling securities issued on 'emerging' stock markets from Delhi to Buenos Aires.

The securities industry has undergone a particularly remarkable transformation over the past decade. Whereas ten years ago Salomon Brothers estimated that 99% of the world's equity trading was done on the exchange where shares had their primary listing, it is reckoned that today one out of every seven equity trades involves a foreigner.

On the London stock market, the world's most international, the figures are much higher. Some 40% of the turnover in shares on the London stock exchange now involves non-UK clients buying non-UK equity. Another quarter involves UK clients buying non-UK equity. There is a much greater awareness among the investment community of business developments outside their home markets.

This, in turn, has fed back to those industries in their home market that used to be the investors' sole focus. They have learnt more about their rivals overseas, and the investment community has become more inclined to think about doing deals across borders. This has made them far more likely to put their traditional domestic customers in touch with potential foreign partners.

The globalisation phenomenon has now spread well beyond the familiar roll call of big names that we spot on the roadside from the airport. The pioneers of globalisation, the Coca-Colas and the Nestlés, firms that were big enough and rich enough to set up their own sales and production operations in a number of different countries in the first flush of enthusiasm for global strategies, have been followed by a new generation.

Many of the firms in this generation have focused on youth markets where international brand awareness is most acute. At the forefront come names like Nike and Caterpillar (the boots, not the earthmovers). But smaller firms like Amazon, the on-line bookshop, and Netscape have been global from their inception. No Silicon Valley start-up builds its business plans today on the assumption that its market is going to stretch no further than New York. Nor does a Hollywood movie producer doing his sums for a new blockbuster.

Use of the Internet promises to shrink the global village and accelerate the process of global shopping even more dramatically. There are already Web sites that offer bank accounts in Switzerland and incorporation in Belize. How long will it be before there are sites selling medicines from Mexico, flowers from Florida, and equity from Ecuador?

This globalisation is creating new markets, but it is creating new uncertainties too. When a number of Asian economies suffered a severe economic downturn in the winter of 1997/98, the domino effect spread not just to other economies in Asia but also to Europe and North America. Not only had large numbers of European and American businesses pinned their hopes of future growth on fast-developing Asia, but some of them had already put a lot of eggs into the Asian basket.

The Organisation for Economic Co-operation and Development (OECD) reckoned that the 1997/98 decline in the economies of the likes of Thailand, South Korea and Indonesia would lop 0.8% off Europe's GNP in 1998 (the equivalent of some $48 billion) and 0.5% off its net exports. Newspapers were full of stories of small western firms whose lost markets in the East were causing them severe difficulties.

Other firms, particularly in industries like car manufacturing, worried that oriental manufacturers would become more competitive in pricing their goods in western markets in order to compensate for their lost markets at home. And that would be sure to put pressure on their western rivals' profitability. 'Our main concern,' said a spokesperson for Philips Electronics, the Dutch multinational, 'is the price policies of competitors exporting to Europe.'

The Asian economic crisis brought home two points in particular:

+ **The inter-relatedness of all parts of the world economy.** The grape pickers of rural Cognac today are deeply affected by how affluent the Japanese middle manager feels; and the assembly-line worker in Ohio needs to keep an eye on the state of the Taiwanese economy. By highlighting this fact the Asian crisis served to increase western companies' concerns about the seemingly uncontrollable nature of today's business life.

+ **The unexpected directions from which business challenges appear.** Few anticipated the downturn in the Asian economies—not even credit rating agencies such as Moody's and Standard & Poor's, whose job it is to be one step ahead of the pack. In an unprecedented confession, the third biggest agency, Fitch IBCA, admitted that it and its competitors had underestimated the spread of 'market contagion' in Asia. They may have also underestimated how global is their own influence today.

New entrants into old markets

The collapse of the walls between industries has not only allowed well-established firms to spread their wings, it has also allowed upstart newcomers to leap into major businesses and seize significant market share in a very short space of time. New entrants, and how to handle them, are a big issue for all industries today.

When Netscape, a complete unknown, launched its browser on the Internet in October 1994 it went from nothing to having 80–90% of the market in less than two years. Two years after it was founded its turnover was $346 million and its market capitalisation $5 billion.

When Davids take on Goliaths in this way (the Goliath in Netscape's case being Microsoft) they frequently do not have the market to themselves for long. The Goliaths fight back. Netscape's market share had fallen to 58% by the third quarter of 1997 after Microsoft packaged its own Internet browser as a free 'extra' with its Windows operating system. Microsoft had grabbed 39% of the market. Likewise Virgin Cola, which set out to take on the giants of the cola business, Pepsi and Coke, found that its market share, which initially in the UK rocketed to 4.7%, fell rapidly as the giants consolidated their distribution and fought back with a number of special promotions.

The possibility of completely new operators appearing suddenly in an industry heightens the feelings of uncertainty. When banks knew that their competitors were confined largely to the ranks of other banks they could keep them in their sights. But now that banks and securities firms risk being reduced, as Citicorp chairman John Reed has put it, to 'a line or two of application code on a network', almost anybody who can gain access to the information systems that produce those codes can become a bank or a securities firm.

Think what that means for institutions that have inherited a vast and expensive branch network. They cannot shed their overheads overnight in order to compete with new entrants that can become low-overhead virtual organisations from their very beginning. They may not even be able to shed their legacy of computer equipment in the time frame necessary to keep the bulk of their business out of the hands of the new entrants.

And the threat from new entrants looks likely to get worse. In future they might not be as visible as they have been so far. Suppose an organisation wants to set up a discount store. In the past, it would have been faced with the daunting task of marketing and advertising the store to get recognition in the marketplace. And after costs like those, most aspiring discounters found it difficult to be a 'discount' anything. Today, on the other hand, they can simply set up a page or two on the Internet and hope that the market finds them.

For instance, the equivalent of a mail-order catalogue can be produced quite cheaply on the Net—and without many of the difficulties associated with that form of selling. If you run out of a particular line of goods, you simply delete it from your electronic 'catalogue'. Then when you have the goods in stock again, you restore them to your pages.

Internet technology has been critical in allowing complete newcomers to challenge old-timers in this way. For example, a Swiss company called Virtual Telecom set up an on-line share price information service in competition with well-established suppliers such as Reuters. By using the Internet the company was ruthlessly able to undercut rivals' prices. Moreover, it allowed the company's customers to access Virtual Telecom's information service from their PCs or from wherever they had access to the Net.

Another example is Amazon.com, the most famous electronic shop in the world. Amazon is a bookseller whose web site is run out of an unprepossessing office in Seattle. It has grown from nothing in a few years to a point where it can claim to be able to supply 2.5 million different titles, far more than any conventional bookshop. Its sales are reckoned to be three times those of the next biggest on-line retailer.

Amazon is more than just an 'e-mail order' supplier of books. It encourages its customers to write on-line reviews of the books that they have bought, and these can then be read by other on-line customers. It is less like a bookshop and more like an information hub where information about books and customers are matched, reshuffled and distributed. Amazon has become so well known that its way of operating has had a strong influence on other developments in Internet shopping.

In on-line markets like these, industry newcomers can become world-wide players overnight. You don't have to be big to be big. The threat to the most established business in an industry can, to repeat John Reed's words, come from 'a line or two of application code on a network'.

Companies looking for ways to respond to new competition would do well to consider a lesson that many boys and girls learnt in the school playground: 'Never take on someone at a game which you can't win'. When a talented new upstart beats you at a game of hopscotch in public you have two options: either you go away and sulk, or you try to change the rules of the game in such a way that you stand a better chance of winning next time. Businesses can't afford to sulk. So they have to re-examine (and if necessary rewrite) the rules of whatever game it is that they want to play.

Customisation

Levi Strauss, the world's biggest jeans-maker, is no sulker. It is in the process of dramatically changing the rules of the game that it plays, namely, the making of jeans. There has never been any shortage of rivals who want to knock Levi Strauss off its pedestal, but the firm has always managed to stay one step ahead of the pack.

The company's latest move is to introduce a service at 200 of its stores that is part of a revolution in marketing. It is a revolution that promises to enable companies to do no less than offer customised services to the masses, offering a partial return to the Victorian hey-day of the bespoke tailor.

Levi Strauss is selling made-to-order jeans by putting a customer's vital statistics into a PC and designing a digital blueprint on the spot.

Levi Strauss is selling made-to-order jeans by putting a customer's vital statistics into a PC and designing a digital blueprint on the spot. The computer file is then transmitted electronically to the company's factory in Tennessee where a robotic tailor cuts a bolt of denim to the design specified in the computer file. The finished product, which costs about $10 more than a mass-produced pair of jeans, is then shipped back to the store within three weeks. Or it can be sent directly to the customer by Federal Express for an extra $5 fee.

Writing in the *Harvard Business Review*, John Deighton, associate professor of marketing at the Harvard Business School, says that evolving technology has the 'ability to put a more human face on marketplace exchanges without losing the scale economies of mass marketing'. In the case of Levi Strauss it might be more appropriate to say that the company is putting 'a more human *shape* on marketplace exchanges'!

In effect, Levi Strauss has found a way to charge a premium in an increasingly commoditised market. A pair of jeans is a pair of jeans is a pair of jeans . . . until it is cut to fit a particular individual's shape. Then it is no longer a commodity; it is a customised product and as such it can fetch a premium price.

In ways like this, technology is doing nothing less than redefine the experience that we call 'shopping'. Not only is it turning mass markets into bespoke ones, it is also emphasising the distinction that market researchers make between 'replacement shopping' and 'pleasure shopping'.

Replacement shopping is the purchasing of things that we consume regularly and that we pick up almost with our eyes closed: the weekly margarine, potatoes or washing powder. For the most part these are commodity products that we don't wish to be customised. Technology—in the shape of the Internet and other 'direct' forms of purchasing—is taking much of the grind out of replacement shopping.

Pleasure shopping, on the other hand, is the sort of thing we do, often with family or friends, on a Saturday afternoon—the buying of Levi's, books, furniture, etc.,—the activity that market researchers say is now the most popular 'leisure pursuit' in many western societies. Technology is enhancing the delights of pleasure shopping by increasing the scope for customising the sort of items that it includes. Buying bespoke jeans creates a relationship between customer and supplier; the choosing of a commodity from a shelf does not.

Technology is doing nothing less than redefining the experience that we call shopping.

Full circle

There is much in all this to please those (like me) who believe that life goes round in circles. The Internet promises to bring back to us the ease and frequency of communication enjoyed by wealthy city dwellers in the nineteenth century, when human messengers, not electronic ones, hurried backwards and forwards like carrier pigeons.

Some manufacturers are purposely echoing the past. Take the latest styling to come out of sexy Italian car manufacturer Alfa Romeo. Called the Nuvola concept, its looks are distinctly (and not entirely by accident) evocative of the classic Alfa racing cars of the 1930s.

But it is not just the look of the car that recalls pre-war years. So does its method of construction. Unusually, the body is dropped onto the completed chassis at the last moment. This enables Alfa to select coachbuilders in different locations to design the bodywork for the car. Not only is this a suitably flexible production process for the 1990s; it also happens to be the way that the cars were manufactured in the 1930s!

Finally, the promise of 'home-working', of being able to work in quiet rural cottages linked electronically to both customers and suppliers, has echoes of the way things were before remorseless economies of scale forced workers together into huge factories. In the pre-Industrial Age, everybody was a 'home worker'. The carpenter chiselled away outside his front door while his neighbour the blacksmith hammered away outside his. We think of it nowadays as a Utopian ideal. But it could be reality in the future. Despite the unique pace of modern day change, we ignore the lessons of history at our peril.

Chapter summary

This chapter has considered some of the major changes that are taking place in businesses today. It has focused first and foremost on the extraordinary way in which traditional boundaries between different industries have been falling. Only a few years ago it would have been unthinkable for supermarkets to be selling banking services, for example. Or for a newcomer in a fast-growing market to gain an 80% share in a couple of years. Yet today these things happen, to nobody's great astonishment.

Behind these changes lie a number of distinct shifts in corporate behaviour, in the way that firms work with other firms, for instance, and in the way that they relate to their customers. I have selected ten of these shifts, the ten which I believe provide the most significant pointers to the future.

My 'Top Ten' consists of:

1   Broadening the range of products and services on offer.
2   Creating new value propositions.
3   Turning themselves into virtual organisations.
4   Getting closer to their customers.
5   Merging, acquiring, and demerging.
6   Forming strategic alliances.
7   Outsourcing.
8   Extending their global reach.
9   Facing competition from new entrants in their markets.
10   Customising their products and services.

Many companies have been encouraged to widen the range of products and services that they sell. Supermarkets provide banking services, for example, and record companies run railways. This is challenging old established firms to find new ways of adding value.

In order to spread themselves as widely as possible companies are creating new corporate structures. Virtual corporations such as Virgin are becoming more common. Companies are also trying to get as close as possible to their customers. Today the customer is king and most organisations know it. Technology is helping them to create new ways of keeping tabs on those customers.

The form in which businesses are getting together is changing. Take-overs are no longer so hostile, and to the traditional mix of M&A, mergers and acquisitions, has been added a D—M&A&D, mergers and acquisitions and demergers. Companies are shedding businesses that they used to own and control. In their place they are forming loose alliances with other companies that they neither own nor control. In some cases, these 'other companies' may even be competitors.

Companies continue to go global, helped by their new networks of alliances and by developments in technology. The Internet and other on-line service providers have boosted eCommerce and have enabled the smallest companies to reach big markets around the globe. Businesses no longer need to be big to be big.

With the walls between industries down, every business may face new competitors that arise from nowhere. And none of them knows where the next competitor will come from. Microsoft has an eye on the financial services business, but with financial services reduced to 'a line or two of application code on a network', the next global banking giant may right now be no more than some software design house near Sausalito.

One way in which companies are hoping to fend off the new competition is by trying to change the rules of their business. Levi Strauss, for example, is attempting to turn its jeans from a commodity product into a customised service. To do this it is using information technology that passes an individual customer's measurements straight to a factory assembly line.

With so many options open to them, companies are having to stand back and ask what businesses they want to be in. The chairman of Revlon once told his sales force that they are not in the business of selling cosmetics; they were 'in the business of selling dreams'. Realising that you are in the business of selling dreams defines to a great extent the options that are open to you.

In the next chapter I take a look at some of the reasons for these remarkable changes, and ask why they are taking place now.

2

Some Reasons for the Fall

IN THIS CHAPTER I EXAMINE WHY THE BOUNDARIES BETWEEN businesses are breaking down in the way I have described in Chapter 1, and why they are breaking down now. Once we understand the reasons for the rapid changes that are taking place in today's business environment, we should be better placed to sketch out some scenarios for the future.

By and large, the forces behind the changes are of two kinds: there are those that are created by the demands of consumers, forces that 'pull' change along in their wake; and there are those that are created by the inventiveness of suppliers—things like new technological developments. This second type of force 'pushes' change ahead of it and sometimes brings about supply-driven revolutions in markets. These two forces together, of pull and push, are the twin engines of industrial change.

At times they may work in opposite directions. For example, there are many cases where companies have prevailed with new products despite a negative initial response from consumers. The Sony Walkman is perhaps the classic example. It was 'pushed' out into the market after early reactions had suggested that there was no consumer 'pull' for the product at all. The rest, as they say, is history.

Similarly Apple got a frosty initial reception for its computer operating system, a system that introduced the revolutionary idea of using icons rather than the written instructions that were familiar to computer users at the time. At one stage the company was very close to abandoning its system. But it persisted, and all interfaces on PCs today are based on user-friendly ideas first pushed onto the market by Apple.

Today, companies are similarly pushing more and more new products and services onto the market, and it is a central message of this book that if your company is waiting to respond to its competitors' lead then it is already losing the game.

The pull of consumers

Let's first consider the pull from consumers. The very nature of consumers has been totally transformed over the past 50 years, and so has their influence on markets. After the Second World War people were happy to see an end to the shortages of basic goods that war had made necessary. Manufacturers could sell almost anything they could produce to customers who were not in a mood to be demanding.

But economic growth rapidly made people much richer and much more demanding. Average family income in the USA increased between two- and three-fold in the 50 years after 1947. On average, today's young workers earn in a day what it took their grandfathers nearly 14 working days to earn. As a consequence, they have very different habits from their grandparents, and very different values.

Today's consumers also just 'are' very different from those of 50 years ago—they're taller, they're older, and almost half of them (the women) have a completely different role in society from that of their grandmothers. Let's consider each of these aspects of consumers in turn: their changing habits; changing values; and changing demographics.

Consumer habits

For a dramatic demonstration of the change in consumer habits, look at the amount that people travel. Fifty years ago very few people took holidays abroad. In 1948 foreign currency was so scarce in Britain that its citizens were banned from going abroad other than for essential commercial purposes. In 1997, by contrast, 57% of British adults had at least one overseas holiday.

This huge increase in foreign travel has had a dramatic effect on consumer's expectations. Holidaymakers come home and wonder why they can't find on their own high street the marvellous things that they found abroad.

One very obvious example of this has been the spread of the American fast-food phenomenon. Europeans, when they began to visit the USA, were impressed with the way that levels of service were being maintained on the other side of the Atlantic. At home they had wearily begun to assume that efficient service in the latter part of the twentieth century (particularly in food and restaurants) was to be something to which only the very wealthy would have access.

Then, suddenly, indigenous restaurants in Europe were having to compete with the likes of McDonald's and Burger King. And either they had to compete as a lower cost, more efficient provider of a burger-type commodity, or they had to move upmarket and provide 'meals'—with all the service add-ons which that implies. It is no exaggeration to say that holidaymakers returning from Miami and other American resorts were the spur to a transformation of Europe's eating habits.

They were also the spur to a radical change in holiday habits. Instead of choosing between Spain and Portugal for their destination, northern Europeans began to find that they were choosing between one resort experience and another. Their choice fell, for example, between a Disney family experience, a beach and water-sports experience, or a city centre sightseeing experience. The country in which the experience was to be gained became a secondary consideration.

There are plenty of other examples of the way in which travel has broadened the consumer's mind and tastes—the Americans' gradual realisation, after the oil crisis, that most of the rest of the world drives around quite comfortably in cars that are half the size of theirs, for example; or the widespread discovery that there are people in many parts of the world who can make wine almost as well, if not (dare we say it?) on occasions even better than the French. They can certainly, travellers soon discovered, sell it more cheaply.

Another significant change in consumer habits has come from the changed nature of their entertainment. Fifty years ago, people flocked out to the cinema; now they stay in and watch television.

At first the spread of television made the rest of the world familiar with a narrow sample of American consumer habits through the sale of programmes like *Dallas* and *Dynasty*. These programmes penetrated even to remote Asian and African villages, where it must have been easy for the villagers to assume that all Americans were millionaires who spent much of their money on lipstick and hair-dryers.

With the development of satellite broadcasting the process took on a new dimension. Satellite television bypassed state-controlled media and their ability to select which foreign programmes could be viewed by whom. Moreover, because it was relatively cheap, satellite television brought forth a host of new broadcasters. And they showed the world a much broader sample of consumers than those portrayed in *Dallas* and *Dynasty*. At Global Business Network they refer to this as 'the democratisation of consumption'.

The spread of television, of course, did much more than influence consumer purchases. The projection of programmes via satellite into Eastern Europe was a major influence on the events that led to the downfall of the communist regimes there and the symbolic fall of the Berlin Wall. East European governments could no longer pretend that they were providing a superior way of life once their citizens could see that capitalism gave its supporters much more than lipsticks and hair-dryers.

Consumer values

While consumer habits changed dramatically, so did their values. Here a major force for change during the period was the so-called 'consumer movement'. Most closely identified with the American pioneer Ralph Nader, the movement set out to prevent defective goods from being foisted onto consumers by irresponsible manufacturers. In the process it made consumers far more aware of the shifting balance of power between them and the producers of goods and services. It was the dawn of an age when the customer became king.

In one sense, Nader was so successful that he put himself and his 'raiders' (as his close supporters were called) out of a job. Consumers in a broad range of western societies soon began to look after their own interests so effectively (or, as voters, got their governments to look after them on their behalf) that they had no more need for organised watchdogs. Today the shoe is almost on the other foot. It is not difficult to feel sympathy for the manufacturer who is expected, for instance, to replace a garment that has dared to shrink after its third wash.

Another major change in consumer values was brought about by the growing concern for the environment. Consumers began to demand not only that products be made so that they could not harm consumers, but also that they be made so that they could not harm the consumers' environment. The percentage of people in the USA who agreed with the statement that 'continuing environmental improvements must be made regardless of cost' rose from 45% to 80% between 1981 and 1990.

Companies like Ben & Jerry's ice cream in the USA and The

Body Shop in the UK have built themselves into major organisations by marketing their environmental concern. Ben & Jerry produces an ice cream called Rainforest Crunch that, according to *The Economist*, 'is chock full of righteously harvested nuts from tribal co-operatives in the Amazon'. That is not a value proposition that would have sold much ice cream 20 years ago. Yet it has been enough to allow Ben & Jerry to rise from nothing and challenge the ice-cream industry giants.

Anita Roddick, founder of The Body Shop, believes that green consumers are going to be increasingly prominent in the future. 'They will be looking,' she says, 'for products that hurt no-one, which damage nothing and which are produced by companies espousing the gentler values that they themselves espouse . . . they will demand information, want to know the story behind what they buy, how it was made, where and by whom. They want to feel sympathy not just with the product but with the process supporting it, how it is manufactured, presented and sold.'

The green movement was itself injected with a sense of urgency by the fall of the Berlin Wall. The West was shocked to discover the horrific environmental damage that had taken place in countries like Russia and East Germany as a result of the communists' hopeless attempts to keep up with capitalism's levels of productivity. In 1989 one river in East Germany literally glowed at night from the cocktail of pollutants flowing through it.

Like the consumer movement before it, the green movement ran out of steam somewhat when the worst abuses had been corrected. Governments have found it hard to deliver on the enthusiastic promises they made at the 1992 'Earth Summit' held in Rio de Janeiro. Of the 108 countries represented there, only three (Germany, Switzerland and the UK) seem likely to meet the commitment to get carbon dioxide emissions down to 1990 levels by the end of the century.

Consumers have been left to tussle with the problem of how to reconcile environmental improvement with economic growth and a continuing rise in their own standard of living. Do they really want to pay a premium of 200% to buy organic carrots? And how are they to get to the supermarket if they can no longer drive there in their fossil-fuel-burning automobile and have a clear environmental conscience?

Regardless of this dampening of consumer enthusiasm, the power of the environmental movement has been considerable. With some fiscal encouragement, sales of unleaded petrol have rocketed. And so-called eco-tourism, where tourists pay to see how beautifully nature is being preserved, is one of the fastest-growing niches in a fast-growing industry. It is even being held responsible for an over-abundance of wildlife in certain parts of Africa. The vexing problem of the motor car remains, but electric power may suggest a solution.

Consumer values are also being changed by a growing tendency for consumers to become more individualistic. In the early decades of this century, the progress of industrialisation was all in one direction—towards mass markets and the production of standardised goods in ever larger quantities in order to reap the benefits of economies of scale. One person's furniture came to resemble everybody else's; so did their car, and their washing machine, and (eventually) their clothes. Producers aimed to make average products at an average cost for an average person. At times it was easy to assume that the world was moving remorselessly towards depressing uniformity.

This trend was halted, however, when consumers began to reassert a desire for personalised products and services. Spurred on by technological change of the sort that has made it possible for Levi's to produce tailor-made jeans, and for BMW to say that it can customise its production to such an extent that very few BMW cars are identical, consumers have demanded greater choice.

Nobody wants to turn up at a party wearing exactly the same clothes as someone else, and for quite a while now the chances of that happening have been diminishing. The chances are that they will continue to diminish.

A common theme running though many of the consumer changes of the past 50 years has been a growing demand for convenience. It is the demand for convenience, for example, that has created supermarkets where shoppers can buy almost everything they require in one location. The demand for convenience has also led to the growth of small 'corner' shops that are open all hours of the day and night, and that charge a premium for the service they provide. And the demand for convenience has encouraged the growth of telemarketing, the direct selling of goods and services by telephone in 'the convenience of your own home'.

Neither supermarkets, 24-hour shopping nor direct marketing have grown up because of their own intrinsic merits. Most of us, given the right circumstances, would rather stroll down a high street chatting with delightful butchers, bakers and greengrocers who draw down their shutters at five in the afternoon (as our grandmothers did). Few of us would choose instead to rush out to a nearby corner shop full of noisy drunken customers at one o'clock in the morning.

This demand for convenience is not one-dimensional and confined to shopping. One of the things that people seek as they become wealthier is more convenient hours of work. Thus we find that people don't want to travel as part of their work as much as they used to. Not only are the attractions less now that people travel outside their work so much more, but travel can be very disruptive to family life, especially when all the adults in the family have full-time jobs.

People are also seeking to work at more convenient hours. Although we are working longer than we used to, we are working less in the wee small hours of the morning. One piece of American research found that whereas in 1973 10% of the male workforce was at work at 3 am in the morning (the hour when the fewest people are at work), by 1991 that figure had fallen to 7%. The extra hours that are being worked these days are being tagged on to the end of the normal working day, or being added at weekends.

This has implications for a number of industries. The 'rush hours' that are a part of life in any large city are becoming more extended, allowing urban transport services to manage their operations more efficiently. And it may leave a question mark over future growth in demand for 24-hour shopping if there are to be fewer people working round the clock. However, the important point about the convenience of 24-hour shopping is that the customer knows that the shop is always open. He does not want the 'inconvenience' of having to remember the hours that it is closed, however short or regular they may be.

Consumer demographics

While the habits and values of consumers have changed beyond recognition over the past 50 years, so has their demographic profile. In particular, people are living longer and they are having fewer children. They want to live in different places, and they want different types of housing. All this has inevitably had a great effect on consumer demand.

In Italy, for example, 17% of the population is today over the age of 65. Twelve years from now that percentage is forecasted to rise to 20%. Yet only 12 years ago the figure was 13.5%. In the UK today, out of every 1000 marriages 13.2 end in divorce. Thirty years ago the figure was 5.9 in 1000.

Similar patterns are to be found in most developed economies. Throughout the countries of the OECD there are now, for example, enough centenarians in reasonably good physical condition for them to be the subject of regular newspaper and magazine articles. We can expect to be in the third decade of the twenty-first century before the last person to have been alive in the nineteenth century dies.

Some of these older people are working longer, but many more are living through prolonged periods of retirement. A manager who takes early retirement in his or her mid-50s—not an exceptional occurrence these days—can expect to have a retirement almost as long as their working life. This has profound implications for the financing of that retirement. Governments are no longer able to fund state pensions that can on their own maintain a reasonable standard of living for their ever-growing number of retirees. This has created enormous market opportunities for the sale of private-sector pensions and other long-term savings instruments.

Medical science is ensuring that people's retirement years are far more active than they used to be. Retirees do not sit at home all day any more. In general they have more time, more money and more energy to spend on leisure activities—hence the growth of new holiday markets such as long-distance cruises. And they have money to spend on ensuring that they remain healthy and active for as long as possible. Hence the great growth in healthcare and related industries.

Another way that the elderly like to spend their money is in migrating. Many active retirees choose to live somewhere else in winter from where they live in summer. In North America they fly down to Florida; in Europe they move to the Mediterranean, to countries like Spain and Portugal. One of the market consequences of this has been to give many summer-only resorts the chance to be all-year-round businesses. Some of them have come to resemble extended old people's homes, exaggerating the distinction between the working young—who by and large live in big busy cities—and the unemployed elderly who gather together in sleepy seaside resorts.

Urbanisation, the movement of workers from the land to towns and cities, has been a major influence on consumer behaviour now for the best part of two centuries. It is still affecting developing countries from Turkey to Thailand in much the same way as it did Victorian Britain when labourers first left 'the land' to work in newly established urban factories. From Istanbul to Bangkok, the average size of families falls as the cost of their accommodation rises.

The size of cities like London, Paris and New York has not changed much over the past 30–40 years as they have been overtaken as the world's biggest concentrations of population by places like Mexico City, Sao Paulo and Mumbai. But the behaviour patterns of the populations of London, Paris and New York have changed greatly.

There, urbanisation has been followed by a sort of de-urbanisation. People have moved back to the countryside and have taken their work with them. These 'home workers' have different demands from their office-based colleagues in the cities. For a start, they use telephone and home delivery services much more, and they need an office or work space in their home, which they prefer to be physically separate from their living space.

At a basic level this is good news for businesses that convert lofts and garages into rooms, for example, or that build flexible garden 'sheds'. On another level, it heralds a different sort of landscape. A recent RIBA (Royal Institute of British Architects) study on the dwellings of the future postulates that groups of houses will soon be built in circular shapes, in the middle of which will be 'work buildings' containing schools and crèches. In these buildings 'workers' will occupy space next to people who are doing completely different things for completely different employers.

Thus a carpenter might spend all day working next to an environmentalist or an author. But since space will be allocated in these buildings according to need, people are unlikely to work at the same desk for two days in a row. The next day the carpenter could have completely different neighbours. Think about the stimulation that this could give to both parties, and think about the synergy that could arise from these new interactions.

In these new 'home-working' environments loyalties will be developed in ways which will have broad implications for business and management. Work relationships will not be created (and destroyed) through physical proximity; rather they will be built up through less intimate forms of communication, particularly via the Internet.

This is likely to strengthen loyalty among communities with a wide diaspora (such as the Chinese, the Jews or the Armenians), and this too could have wide commercial implications. Non-interest-paying Islamic banks, for instance, may make more commercial sense as Net-based institutions serving a global niche market than as physical branches on carefully chosen street corners.

Some of the biggest changes in society in recent years, however, have followed from the almost universal shift in the role of women. This has led, in the first instance, to a far greater number of women going out to work. The growth of the double-income family, where both husband and wife work full time, has created new market needs and opportunities. Market researchers have defined a new category called 'Dinkies'—family units that have 'a dual income and no kids'. Dinkies have all sorts of special needs—mostly related to convenience—that their substantial incomes mean that they are well able to meet.

Almost single-handedly they have invented the short weekend break; their tight schedules giving them no time for anything longer. And when they came to want their weekends to be healthy too they encouraged thousands of health farms to spring up to meet their demand.

Dinkies also wanted to give dinner parties for other dinkies, but they didn't have the time to prepare impressive meals. So the market for pre-prepared convenience foods grew to meet that demand. Then, as their incomes grew, these well-off couples moved on to taking their friends out for dinner. The growth in the number of people eating out in restaurants has been not far short of phenomenal in recent years.

When these couples chose to have children—in general, at a far later age than their parents—their needs changed again, and they were different needs from those of their parents. Mothers took short spells of maternity leave, but then wanted to put their children in the care of nannies or of day-care centres so that they could get back to work.

Paralleling this growth in double-income households has been a growth in single-parent households. The ever-rising divorce rate in western societies has given birth to large numbers of single-parent families whose special needs have influenced markets and governments. Single-parent families tend to fall into the lower income brackets, but they still need things like pre-school child care so that the parent can continue to work. They also create a greater demand for smaller housing units.

The push of suppliers

Just as I have subdivided into three the forces that have been pushing consumers to change—new habits, new values and shifting demographics—so I subdivide into three the forces that have been pulling suppliers to change: increasing competition leading to overcrowded markets; deregulation leading to new market opportunities; and the accelerating pace of change that has left firms with no time to rest on their laurels.

Just as consumers have changed beyond recognition over the past 50 years, so have suppliers. In 1947, for example, half the office buildings in the UK were deemed by the National Federation of Professional Workers not to be up to a 'proper and decent standard'. Hand-operated mechanical adding machines were the most sophisticated technology that workers could hope for. IBM was still experimenting with a machine that it called Eniac, the Electronic Numerical Integrator and Computer. 'It is still in its infancy,' said one of the scientists working on it at the time. And he added, with a flash of insight: 'The multiplicity of problems which it can handle has not yet been defined'.

Increasing competition

One of the most striking features of suppliers today is the fact that they are invariably operating in markets which are very crowded—not just crowded with customers but crowded with suppliers too. Whereas 30 years ago consumers could choose between three or four shampoos and three or four breakfast cereals, today there are hundreds of shampoos and breakfast cereals available. Consumers are literally spoilt for choice.

This overcrowding is forcing companies to move elsewhere, both geographically and in terms of the range of products and services that they offer. An indicator of the extent to which they have looked for new markets abroad is the level of foreign direct investment (FDI), the amount that they spend on buying and starting businesses in other countries. FDI by the world's major corporations grew astronomically in the 1980s, and scarcely stopped for breath in the 1990s. FDI by companies from the 26 member nations of the OECD rose by over 50% in 1995 alone.

Overcrowding has forced companies to look harder for ways to create new markets. New emphasis has been placed on research and development, and particularly on development. Firms have redefined traditional products in order to make them appeal to new markets. The drugs company, SmithKline Beecham (SKB), for example, has shifted the market for one of its best-known products.

Lucozade used to be a distinctively coloured fizzy drink that gave kids energy after colds and flu. As such it was more or less aligned with SKB's product range. But Lucozade has now been repositioned as a sports drink. No longer sold as something for the frail and sick, it is being marketed as quite the opposite—a drink that gives a (perfectly legal) boost to sportsmen and women.

At Andersen Consulting, we foresee a way that today's suppliers will seek to avoid overcrowding: instead of providing customers with a means to an end, a marquee in which to hold their wedding reception, for instance, they will increasingly offer a service that seeks to satisfy a customer's overall 'intention'—their desire for a particular experience—a Hawaiian style wedding, say, with the garlands, the honeymoon on Waikiki and everything else that such an intention implies.

In the example of the mortgage loan considered earlier, the supplier who seeks to add value to the basic commodity product (the loan) will do so by combining it with services that help to satisfy the consumers' overall intention. In this case the intention would be to move house, and anyone wishing to be an 'intention matcher' in this business will need to integrate services like those of a real estate agent or a furniture remover to their original mortgage lending.

The same trend can be seen at the supermarkets. They are trying to satisfy people's intentions by helping them to create an exciting meal, rather than merely to buy basic foodstuffs. Increasingly they place things that are eaten with each other close together on their shelves—spices for mulling wine, for instance, in the liquor section rather than in the spice department; sweet and sour sauce next to the noodles, not next to the ketchup.

This development could still have a good way to go. As more and more people eat out in restaurants they are getting accustomed to choosing from sophisticated menus. It may not be long before we see a supermarket in which customers, when they first enter, are taken into a sort of café where they are invited to read through a list of meals—just as they would in their favourite restaurant.

They will then be asked to choose (from this 'menu') those meals that they would like to eat over the next few days. A computer-generated list of the ingredients required to cook them will be created—along with the recipes; whereupon, armed with a list, consumers can set off to do their shopping.

Regulation

The impact of regulation and deregulation in reshaping markets cannot be ignored. Under the influence of the Reagan and Thatcher governments in the USA and the UK, the 1980s became a decade of widespread deregulation. Industries from airlines to telecoms and banking were turned inside out by new regulations as to what they could and couldn't do. In general, deregulation meant that more firms could do what had previously been the preserve of an exclusive few. This had a very direct effect in bringing down long-established walls between industries.

Despite this spate of deregulation, however, regulators continue to have a powerful impact on markets. In countries (like the UK) where deregulation was accompanied by a widespread selling off to the private sector of state-owned monopolies, the privatisation process involved setting up a bevy of new regulators. Deregulation in one industry is being matched by re-regulation in another.

The job of these new regulators is to watch over the private-sector monopolies and oligopolies that have replaced the state-owned ones, and to see that consumers' interests are protected. They have considerable powers and can, for example, fix price rises.

Well-established regulators—such as the USA's Food and Drug Administration (the FDA)—continue to wield a powerful influence over a number of major industries. And so do anti-trust authorities such as the US Justice Department and the EC Commission. The Justice Department has flexed its muscles in recent years with no less a company than Microsoft, wanting it to unbundle its Internet browser from its computer operating system.

Both American and European regulators have been involved in determining the future shape of the airline industry and (more recently) of the accounting industry—the latter through their consideration of the monopoly implications of the merger between Coopers & Lybrand and Price Waterhouse.

Another form of deregulation, the deregulation of the labour markets, has also had an influence on suppliers. The declining influence of rigid trade unions, for instance, has freed workers to do things that might be deemed to fall outside their original contracts of employment. Add to that new flexible production processes which have enabled factories to make one thing today and another thing tomorrow, and it is easy to see how companies can have their fingers in many more pies than used to be available to them.

No one foresees a world in which market regulation is not a force to be reckoned with. All of our scenarios for the future (Chapters 4–8) take it fully into account, although each of them foresees it developing very differently.

Pace of change

Overcrowded and flustered. The rapid pace of change is giving companies less and less time to enjoy any competitive advantage that they may have in a particular market. The Dutch electronics giant Philips started selling a highly sophisticated car navigation system in 1997. Satellite based, it contains a voice message that directs drivers to their destination. If the vehicle takes a wrong turning the system recalibrates itself to take account of its new direction. It is a product that is going to make every taxi-driver in the world as efficient as a London cabby with 'the knowledge'.

It sounds like futuristic stuff, sufficiently advanced to give Philips the market to itself for some time to come. But it was at most a matter of months before a competing system began to emerge. Philips had only a very small window of opportunity in which to reap the rewards of its invention.

Even when a company has a seemingly impregnable market position it cannot rest on its laurels and allow invention to slow up. Intel, the leading manufacturer of semiconductors for PCs, had its famous '486' chip ready for the market before it had launched the 486's predecessor, the 386. Likewise, by the time the 486 was launched, its replacement (the Pentium chip) was already on the production line. Now the Pentium II has been launched and its successor, the Merced, is already in production.

Another example of the need for speed in markets that can change so swiftly comes from the experience of an American journalist who a couple of years ago was preparing an article about the threat to long-distance telecoms companies such as AT&T from calls made over the Internet. At the time (the end of 1996) over 15 million households in America had access to the Net, and the number was doubling every year. The journalist's theme was that the Internet looked set to destroy long-distance calls, the bedrock of AT&T's profits.

As he finished writing his story, however, somebody told the journalist that AT&T had just announced that it was about to launch an Internet service. The American telecoms giant had decided that if you can't beat them, join them. The writer tore up his story and set to work on something else.

But then he went to Silicon Valley on another project and he was telling a scientist there about the article that he had torn up. 'You were crazy to tear it up,' said the scientist. 'In the time that it takes AT&T to launch an Internet service something else will arise that will again threaten to completely undermine its business.' So the journalist resurrected his old article, fine-tuned it, and sent it off to his paper.

The pharmaceuticals industry has been heavily influenced by the need for products to get to market more quickly. The time that new drugs have on the market before their patents expire (at which time they can be produced by anybody) is getting shorter and shorter. Some of this is due to the protracted process in getting regulatory approval for each new drug. The large number of mergers in the industry can be partly explained by the companies' need to reap economies of scale in their R&D.

These pressures have led a number of drug companies to look not at new products but at new businesses. Firms such as Zeneca are moving beyond the manufacture of traditional drugs and into the business of running hospitals and health-care units.

In industrial history there are plenty of instances of firms that came too early to market with a product. The Nottingham Building Society, a small UK financial institution, launched a home banking service some 15 years ago. It was a videotext-based service way ahead of its time, and it never took off. Similarly the French have been experimenting with 'smart cards'—cards with a semiconductor in them—for a similar length of time, initially in healthcare applications. As with home banking, only recently have they begun to come into more general use. But the number of products appearing before their time is diminishing as rapidly as the pace of change is accelerating.

Another major change in markets has been in the way in which goods and services are delivered to the customer. Mail order, for instance, has been transformed. In the USA, it

developed in the early years of this century as companies such as
Sears Roebuck sought to overcome the great distances between
the farms of the Mid-West and half-decent shops. In the UK,
where distances are not such an obstacle, mail order grew because
it provided an early form of consumer credit.

The boost it has received in recent years has come from a
different direction: mail order has become a convenient way of
shopping for middle-class, urban-dwelling double-income families.
Catalogues sent through the post with growing frequency sell
everything from teak garden benches to Chilean wine aged in oak.

Another revolution in distribution is set to come from the
rapid take-up of the home computer. On-line shopping is already
well beyond the stage of test marketing in many countries, and is
sure to go much further. The Consumer Direct Co-operative, a
consortium of 31 major companies (including Coca-Cola and
Nabisco, and led by Andersen Consulting) has estimated that by
the year 2007 there will be between 15 million and 20 million
households in the USA alone who are doing their shopping on-
line. These 15–20 million households will be spending some $85
billion a year on-line on food and other products.

One interesting byproduct of the Consumer Direct Co-
operative's research is an estimate that on-line shopping will
replace at least half of the 17 shopping trips that the average
American citizen makes each month. That should have a
balancing effect on other changes that point to worrying increases
in the future use of the automobile.

The impact of the Internet will be magnified by new
technology in the pipeline. At the moment, information is pushed
out onto the Net more or less indiscriminately by suppliers. In
time, however, consumers will increasingly be able to pull out the
information that they need as the search engines that enable them
to find out specific information for themselves become more
sophisticated.

For example, in a few years time a small business operating in a market where there is a choice of suppliers of electric power might be able to post its electricity requirements onto the Net. Suppliers by then will have established search engines that will roam the Net in order to pick up invitations to tender such as these. They will thus be able to send an electronic quote almost immediately, and the small business will be able to choose a supplier after comparing quotations.

Today we can already find agents like Andersen Consulting's BargainFinder that scour the Net for quantifiably comparable products—from books and CDs to steel—and then tell buyers where they can find the cheapest price. These new market efficiencies are challenging the traditional value chains and creating opportunities for new entrants. They will soon be fundamentally shifting market structures.

Even industries that are themselves an integral part of the developments in IT are being turned upside down by it. Andrew Grove, chief executive of Intel, the $17 billion semiconductor manufacturer whose chips are to be found in more than 70% of all IBM and compatible PCs, wrote in *Forbes* magazine in September 1996:

> '*If software developed for the Internet will run on anybody's microprocessors, that would open our business to competition by a number of players who today are not really players because their chips don't run the software that PC-users now predominantly use. Our product could be commoditised.*'

Information-based industries that have a physical place of business (like a stock exchange or a bank branch) are particularly vulnerable to developments in IT. Competitors that are unburdened with 'legacy assets' such as shops and branches can arise almost overnight. They can undercut traditional suppliers to such an extent that they are often able to build up substantial market share in next to no time.

Rapid developments in information technology have had a major impact on the structure of many industries. But their impact has been uneven, affecting some industries more than others.

I have found that the influence of IT varies in line with two things in particular:

+ **The position of the industry on the value chain**. Industries that are positioned closer to the consumer (retailing, banking, etc.) tend to be more affected by changes in IT than those earlier in the value chain (steel making or coal mining, for example).

+ **The information content of the product**. There is a significantly greater impact on products and services that are primarily information-based than there is on products and services that are essentially tangible. Financial services, for example, is an information-based industry that is being revolutionised by IT. Coal mining is not.

Consider an old-established financial service such as stockbroking. An information-based business that has been kept in the hands of an oligopoly for centuries by the skilful manipulation of information, stockbroking has been completely revolutionised by technology. The coming of IT has thrown the business wide open.

For a start, stock exchanges no longer need physical 'floors' now that trading in securities is carried out via the telephone and the computer. The London Stock Exchange, by far the largest in Europe, has introduced a combined trading and information system that was designed by Andersen Consulting. Called Sequence, the system is turning the telephone-based London market into a fully electronic screen-based market.

Such systems—the future shape of all stock exchanges—diffuse trading away from a single central floor, and they imply dramatic changes among the firms that are allowed to participate in the new-style trading. That's not to say that the old trading floors are completely redundant. The London Stock Exchange rented its former trading floor in the summer of 1996 for a party to celebrate the launch of Sequence!

In the USA markets have gone one step further. Andrew Klein, a young entrepreneur, has set up a company called Wit Capital Corp, a New York 'investment bank' dedicated to arranging public offerings and sales of securities on the World Wide Web. Klein plans to link up with on-line brokerage firms in order to create a full-blown securities market on the Web.

'There is so much interest in using the Internet for stock trading,' says Robert Colby, deputy director at the SEC, the US securities market regulator, 'that I imagine that at some point someone is going to submit a proposal for a highly developed market that would be the same as an exchange as we perceive it.'

It is not just new developments in information technology that have been revolutionising industries. Other new technologies have also had a significant impact. Defence industry research, boosted in particular by the US defence department's Cold War strategy of spending so much that the Russians simply could not keep up, has thrown up a range of technologies that have changed industrial processes and acted as a spur to new products that industry has pushed onto the market.

The space race has also thrown up a host of new technologies that industry has developed for the benefit of consumers. Much of the miniaturisation of IT, for example, was driven by the need of the US space agency NASA to fit the electronics that it was about to send hurtling into space into ever smaller (and lighter) packages. The Strategic Defense Initiative (or 'Star Wars program')—the US military technology development programme that finally made the Russians admit that they could not stay in the arms race—has brought forth many beneficial results including: improvements in flame-retardant and heat-protective clothing for fire fighters and the possibility of an electromagnetically propelled train that can run on adapted, but otherwise conventional track.

New satellite technology threatens to transform a market as stable as that for taxis. Once upon a time taxis used to gather on ranks, where customers knew they could be found. Or they were hailed on the street. Then, quite suddenly, their business was radically altered by the widespread introduction of in-car two-way radio systems. Taxis could be 'hailed' even when customer and car were not in sight of each other.

Now another revolution is on the horizon, brought about by the development of computer-based routing systems that not only advise drivers on congested routes to avoid, but also tell them where their passengers' desired destination is, and what is the best way to get there.

Why now?

Finally, we are left to ask why is all this change taking place now? And why is it all so much more frenetic than it used to be? The answer to these questions lies partly in the cyclical nature of things—at certain points in history change occurs very rapidly, while at other times societies can stagnate for decades with very little change. And it lies partly in the sheer number of forces that are operating in business today, many of which I have considered above.

The effect of these forces is not linear, because the strength of each one is not independent of the others. As I hope I have shown, they interact with each other in entirely unexpected ways and bring about entirely unexpected changes. It is as if a number of tornadoes were meeting at one point. Their combined impact would be extraordinary, even if each one on its own were nothing special.

Many of the forces for change, however, are quite extraordinary in their own right. Take the speed at which things get superseded. The rate of obsolescence in the computer industry is phenomenal. With the PC, for example, consumers want the latest model incorporating the newest and most powerful chip. They pass on their old models, maybe, to their children because the second-hand market for computers is so thin that they can get nothing for it even if it is in pristine condition.

But their children are buying computer games whose shelf life is even shorter than that of the PC on which they play the game. (The average shelf life of a computer game today is about six months.) The children then discover that the hot new computer game that they got for their birthday only runs on the latest most powerful model of computer. So their parents have to buy another—or risk not gaining access to their own. And so it goes on, faster and faster. A combination of forces as powerful as this is enough to make any business dizzy.

It makes it difficult enough to analyse and understand events in the past. But it seems to eliminate the possibility of having any prior understanding of how things might be in the future. It is the central message of this book, however, that this need not be the case. There is a way to move forward on reasonably firm ground. The next chapter describes where to find it.

Chapter summary

In this chapter I have looked at some of the reasons behind the collapse of boundaries between industries, and have divided the reasons into three:

1 Those related to changes in the nature and behaviour of consumers.

2 Those related to changes in markets; and

3 Those related to changes within industries themselves.

Among those relating to changes in consumer behaviour, I have mentioned the growth in the purchasing power of individuals in all societies since the Second World War. This has turned consumers from docile recipients of whatever producers offered them into demanding drivers of market change. Yesterday the customer was the serf; today he is the king.

Greater wealth has led to greater travel, which has enabled consumers to taste a wider range of goods and services. Choice has been further expanded by the growth of advertising and of television, which makes consumers more easily aware of new products as and when they are launched.

Other major changes in consumer behaviour were brought about by things like the consumer movement, a movement almost synonymous with its pioneer Ralph Nader, and the green movement which reflected growing concern about industrial pollution of the environment.

Individuals also grew tired of standardised products that made their homes all look the same, and they began to demand individualised tailor-made products and services.

Huge shifts in the demographic profile of society have had an enormous effect on consumer demand. People are living longer and are in better health than ever before. And they are having fewer children and living in smaller units. In some countries populations are still shifting away from agricultural land and into cities; in other countries they are moving away from the cities and into rural 'work spaces'.

The changing role of women in society has also had a dramatic effect on the patterns of consumption. Not only do more and more women go out to work full time, but they are getting married later, having children later, and very frequently getting divorced. The single-parent family is a fast-growing social unit.

Behind many of the changes in consumer demand in recent years has been a search for convenience. People no longer have time to shop in extended high streets like their grandmothers. Supermarkets, 24-hour shopping and less anti-social working hours have all grown on this need for convenience.

Market changes that have influenced the fall of industrial boundaries in recent years include the sheer overcrowding of markets. Where once there was a choice of three or four shampoos, now there is a choice of hundreds. Consumers are literally spoilt for choice.

Another major change has been the shorter time in which companies can enjoy any competitive advantage. Original products that appear today are followed by a host of rivals tomorrow.

Markets have also changed dramatically in the way that goods and services are distributed to consumers. Mail order and eCommerce threaten to overturn traditional marketing and sales channels.

In their search for more space in the marketplace companies are attempting to redefine their markets. They are looking to satisfy a wider range of consumer needs by focusing on consumer 'intentions' rather than the underlying elements which support those intentions; e.g. a useful retirement which includes such elements as a pension and retirement home.

Markets have also been greatly affected by changes in regulation and deregulation. While in many industries deregulation has been the order of the day, in some state-owned industries that have been sold off to the private sector, re-regulation has been the usual pattern.

Finally, suppliers themselves have been changed by a number

of things, but by far the most powerful has been the very rapid developments in technology. Information technology has had a particularly powerful effect, an effect that varies with the position of an industry on the value chain and with the information content of its products. Industries (such as financial services) that are close to the consumer and have a high information content are being revolutionised by IT. Others, like coal mining, are not.

Other technological developments have also had remarkable effects. Many of them—like miniaturisation and global positioning systems, for example—have grown out of military research and the race to win the Cold War.

This technological commotion has given birth to the virtual organisation, one freed from constraints of time, place and form. Virtual organisations are able to add value in almost any industry, crossing boundaries at will whenever there is a clear commercial opportunity.

Finally I ask why all this change is happening now, and conclude that it is a result of the concurrence of a number of powerful forces. It is rather like the coming together of a number of tornadoes, none of them particularly destructive on their own. But put together they represent an awesome threat to anything in their path.

3

Predicting the Unpredictable

IN THE EXECUTIVE SUMMARY I QUOTED AN OLD ARAB PROVERB: 'He who predicts the future lies, even if he tells the truth.' I quote it again here just to emphasise that it is a fundamental point that all of us must come to terms with. Whatever we do we cannot predict the future. It is, and will always remain, unknown.

Inevitably, this presents the businessman or woman with a terrible dilemma. For firms must make decisions today in anticipation of what might happen in the future. For example, a TV manufacturer would want to know how many digital televisions they should be producing 3–5 years from now.

But as the ancient Arabs uncomfortably remind us, we cannot know now what that demand will be way into the future. Even the answer to an apparently simple (and fundamental) business question such as, 'How long will the American economy continue to boom?' is beyond us.

And so we cannot make a 'correct' decision today about what our investments should be. And if our decisions today are logically and irrefutably going to be wrong, why bother trying to get them right? Indeed, you might ask, why bother making them at all.

The answer to this troubling quandary lies in the fact that the future is not just waiting to happen. To some extent it is ours to be made. 'He who makes the future controls it,' goes an old saying. Whatever decisions we make now are going to shape the future to some extent, which in itself helps to ensure that they are the right decisions.

One tool that we can use to guide us is called scenario planning.

Scenario planning is designed to help companies and the people who work in them to take a longer-term view of their business in a world of increasingly rapid and unpredictable change. It is a tool that has been (and continues to be) used by some of the largest corporations in the world. Among them are Royal Dutch/Shell, which was largely responsible for the early development of scenario planning, Motorola, IBM, AT&T, Disney and Andersen Consulting.

The scenario planning process involves bringing together a number of senior executives from an organisation and, basically, encouraging them to fantasise about the future of their business. But this process cannot be allowed to be entirely random or else it degenerates into absurdity. In practice, for it to be most fruitful, it needs to be quite tightly structured, and for this purpose it can be helpful to introduce an outsider to direct the discussion.

The process has to start with a prolonged consideration by the senior executives of an organisation about how they think key changes in society, economics, politics and technology are going to affect their markets. They might consider, for example, the impact of the ageing of populations in western societies; or the economic prospects of Russia and China; or the return of right-wing nationalist governments in major economies of the West; or (inevitably) the growth of the Internet and of eCommerce.

As with all tools, scenario planning is only as good as the people who use it. So it is critical that the right people be chosen to take part in the process, and that they all understand what it is about. It is basically aiming to broaden their minds so that they think about market possibilities that would never otherwise have occurred to them.

Out of the process, for which an initial session can last for as long as two whole days, the group will be aiming to draw up a list of those issues that are going to have the most impact on their business, and of those whose outcome is the most uncertain. These issues will form a basis for sketching out some rough scenarios of the future.

After the initial session, the executives go on to consider in greater detail the implications of those issues that they have identified as being most crucial to their business. This involves a combination of more detailed research into key trends, and further thought about the implications of the key drivers of change that they have identified.

Some time later, the same group of executives need to return for another two-day session in which they attempt to flesh out the scenarios more fully and begin to focus on the implications for their organisation of each one of those scenarios. At the same time they attempting to identify some early warning signals—things that, should they happen, would be strong indicators that one specific scenario was beginning to predominate (in the real world) over any other.

The history of scenario planning

Scenario planning grew out of the thinking by a number of top companies (and particularly by Royal Dutch/Shell) about the corporate planning function. It has been driven largely by a combination of two things:

✦ widespread dissatisfaction with existing methods of thinking about the future; and
✦ growing attachment to the idea that business can make better use of the non-rational side of human nature.

Corporate planning, in some senses, has existed for as long as corporations themselves. The managers of William Blake's 'satanic mills' had to take some view of future demand when they imported their raw materials, and over the years this process of 'taking a view' has become more and more formalised. The disruptions of two world wars to some extent postponed the time when it became a fully integrated part of corporate activity.

By the 1960s, however, corporate planning had well and truly come into its own. There was widespread acceptance in the western world of the need for companies to look ahead and to try and trim their sails according to the way the wind was going to blow. In the communist world, of course, it was a case of leave it up to the Kremlin. Indeed, a crucial distinction between the two systems was the communists' insistence that 'Nanny State' knew best, and the capitalists' insistence on the responsibility of each individual corporation for its own fate.

In the 1970s, however, there was a growing frustration with the traditional tools of corporate planning. More and more organisations came to realise how impossible it was to make meaningful predictions based on what was never much more than an extrapolation from the past. Largely as a consequence of this frustration, there was a general reversion against the whole idea of corporate planning. Companies that did not actually close their corporate planning departments invariably downgraded them and reduced their access to the board.

Two of the most significant events during this time were the oil crises that occurred in 1973 and 1978. Previously, most economies had seen a slow gentle progression from the hardships of war to the comforts of a modern consumer society. But the oil price hikes dramatically and painfully brought home to businesses how vulnerable they were to sudden discontinuities in their markets, and that far from being exceptional, such discontinuities were commonplace. The unusually smooth path of economic progress since the Second World War had lulled companies into forgetting that fact.

For the most part, the charts that they had pored over had shown things moving in straight lines, and this led them to believe that the future would be a continuation of the past...but with more of it. Even when the charts did not move in straight lines, their curves seemed to be gentle and predictable.

The OPEC-induced oil crisis of November 1973 (when the price of a barrel of oil rose from $2.90 to $11.65 per barrel in the space of three months) shocked corporate planners into realising that there was something lacking among the tools available to them. Scenario planning entered the picture in a major way because it was seen to have helped the Royal Dutch/Shell company to manage its business rather better than its competitors following the first big oil-price hike.

At the beginning of the 1970s Shell had been a bit ahead of the pack in realising that there was something unsatisfactory about its planning process. As a consequence, it had asked its planning department to take a critical look at the company's planning systems and to find ways, as it put it, of 'coping with unpleasant discontinuities in markets'.

At the head of its planning department at the time were two powerful personalities. One of them, Pierre Wack, was an intellectual Belgian who had been persuaded to give up the editorship of a Franco–German philosophy magazine in order to join Shell. The other, Ed Newland, was an extrovert Argentinean who enjoyed gambling.

Within their department they had a group of managers who came from ten different countries and from at least ten different disciplines, ranging from accounting to nuclear physics. Out of this unlikely mix emerged a dramatically new way of thinking about corporate planning.

In a 1985 article in the *Harvard Business Review* ('The Gentle Art of Re-perceiving') Pierre Wack described Shell's scenario planning process at the time. What distinguished it from other companies' analysis, he said, was not technical. Shell just had a completely different philosophy.

'Almost by definition,' wrote Wack, 'scanning the business environment and crystallising the findings in a set of scenarios means dealing with a world outside the corporation. For example, the evolution of demand, supply, prices, technology, competition, business-cycle changes, and so forth. But this is only a half-truth and dangerous because there is another half.

'Because the raw materials of scenarios are made from this stuff of outer space, it is not realised that more is needed: scenarios must come alive in inner space, the manager's microcosm where choices are played out and judgement exercised.

'Scenarios deal with two worlds; the world of facts and the world of perceptions. They explore for facts but they aim at perceptions inside the heads of decision-makers. Their purpose is to gather and transform information of strategic significance into fresh perceptions.

'This transformation process is not trivial—more often than not it does not happen. When it works, it is a creative experience that generates a heartfelt "Aha" from your managers and leads to strategic insights beyond the mind's reach.'

Any scenario planning process is a journey in search of discoveries and of strategic insights. It needs to draw on a wide range of disciplines and interests. The recommended reading list of Global Business Network, one of the world's leading scenario planners, includes things such as Alexis de Tocqueville's *Democracy in America*, for instance, as well as Peter Senge's *The Fifth Discipline*. And it also includes Giuseppe Tomasi's sweeping tale of Sicilian family life—*The Leopard*—and the video of John Ford's movie, *The Man who Shot Liberty Valance*.

It is a process that demands that participants think the unthinkable. After the second 1970s price hike in 1979, Shell went on to use the same methodology to look at what might happen in exactly the opposite situation—i.e. if the oil price should fall through the floor. At the time nobody within the company honestly believed that it would. But they started to explore the possibility as part of a wider review of the impact of the Soviet Union (as it then was) on their future business. And in one of the scenarios within that review the Soviet republics find such vast quantities of easily accessible oil that they completely undermine the power of OPEC.

So when the oil price did actually plummet from $23 to $8 a barrel between January and July 1986, Shell had already found the time to think of what the implications of such an event might be for its business, and of what it might do to minimise the damage to it. Moreover, it had drawn up a list of those events that could reasonably be expected to be suggesting that oil prices were heading in a steeply downward direction. This meant not only that it was quicker off the starting blocks than its competitors when the fall actually came, but that it was actually up and running before the others had even left their blocks.

Old-fashioned forecasting

Old-fashioned forecasting is constantly attempting to focus on certainties, and to tie down those things that we feel we do know about the future—the imminent introduction of new government legislation, say, or the opening of new plant and distribution channels. Forecasting falls short largely because it pushes uncertainties to one side. They cannot be handled within its framework, so it chooses to ignore them.

But uncertainties are going to be the biggest influence on the future. So it is not very helpful to try and ignore them.

One of the certainties that forecasters assume, and on which they rely heavily, is that of demographics. Demographics are comforting to forecasters because they seem able to tell us the size of future markets. For example, the number of people who will be of pensionable age in the year 2020 can be foretold with reasonable certainty now—failing the outbreak of some major pandemic or the start of another world war.

Likewise, as fertility rates tend to be stable in mature societies, so demographers can also forecast with a considerable degree of certainty the number of teenagers who will be alive in the United States in the year 2020.

Or can they? In fact, the certainty of demographics is sometimes an illusion. In 1988, for example, the US census bureau predicted that in 60 years' time the population of the United States would be much the same as it was then. Fertility rates would continue to decline, as they had been doing for a number of years, and the smaller number of young people that would exist as a consequence would balance any increase in the elderly that arose from the gradual lengthening of life expectancy that had been experienced during the 1980s.

A mere four years later, however (by 1992), the census bureau was painting a rather different picture of America's population 60 years hence. By then, it said, the population would have increased by some 50% from its 1992 level. That meant that in the space of a mere four years, the official monitor of the American population had made an upward adjustment in its estimate of what that population would be in 60 years' time of almost 120 million people. From one census to the next, the character of the American economy of the future had been completely transformed. From being a mature, slow-growing elephant, it had become a dynamic, fast-growing 'tiger'.

The census bureau had been forced to make its massive adjustment because of a number of quite dramatic changes that had taken place in the outside environment in the intervening years. For one, the rates of immigration into the United States had picked up dramatically, and the bulk of that immigration was coming from Latin countries to the south. In those countries, fertility rates are far higher than in the United States itself, and immigrant communities tend to retain the fertility rates of their old culture long after they have settled in a new environment.

Moreover, the bureau had found that it had underestimated the effects of medical advances in healthcare on the average life span. The number of centenarians in the United States (and elsewhere) was increasing by unexpected leaps and bounds.

This reminded the bureau that it lives in a world of uncertainty, and that great uncertainties can have great impact. We can all of us dodge around obstacles that we see, but what happens when we are suddenly hit on the back of the head by a swinging crane? It may not be too pleasant to contemplate, but shouldn't we at least recognise the possibility and spend a little time considering its consequences?

Such a process should help to throw up warning signs. What would indicate that there were swinging cranes in the area, for example . . . a lot of men wearing hard hats? Or passers-by looking upwards and in the same direction? When you spot one of these early warning signs in real life, the planning that you have done will trigger off a list of actions that you should then take . . . starting, in this particular instance, with 'Duck'!

The failings of forecasting

There is no shortage of examples demonstrating how misguided can be any assumption that the future is going to be a simple continuation of the past. In one famous case some of the best minds in IBM got together at Boca Raton in Florida for a brainstorming session. Their aim was to anticipate the future of the personal computer market, a market that had only just begun to open up. At the time (1980), it could be argued that nobody in the world had more knowledge of computers and the computer industry than the people gathered in that room. IBM had a seemingly unassailable position in the computer market, comparable to the position that Microsoft has today in software.

The Boca Raton meeting took place soon after the upstart Apple Computer company had bought a series of full-page advertisements in national newspapers in order to welcome IBM 'to the revolution', the revolution in question being the one brought about by the introduction of the PC. Although the Apple company claimed to have realised early on that PCs were indeed going to revolutionise almost every business on earth, not it nor anybody else realised quite what a revolution they were about to unleash.

And certainly not the brains of IBM gathered in Boca Raton. For they then collectively made a forecast that the world market for PCs would reach some 265,000 by the year 1990. As they saw it from the perspective of 1980, that was a huge leap.

And it was easy to think at the time that they were sticking their necks out to make such a wild forecast. For there were then probably no more than 70,000 computers in total on the whole face of the earth.

The fact that by 1990 there were some 60 million personal computers on desktops from Menlo Park to Hyde Park does not reflect particularly badly on IBM's experts. It just shows how ill equipped they were to think about revolutions and their impact. All their training had prepared them to think merely of evolution—even though they did work for the biggest and most technologically advanced corporation in the world.

Likewise, it did not enable them or their colleagues to see that there would be profit to be made from developing their own operating systems rather than letting a young lad called Bill Gates supply them with his. And it did not enable them either to see that they should buy the microchip architecture that was being offered to them at that time by a small company called Intel. How were they to know that between 1987 and 1998 Intel was to grow from being 256th on *Fortune*'s list of the Top 500 firms in America (and deeply in the red) to being 38th on the list with annual profits of almost $7 billion?

In another less publicised example from about the same time, a major American supplier of equipment to the oil industry set out to forecast the number of active rigs that there would be in the United States in the year 1990. Typically, the company started by looking at growth in the recent past, and it saw that the number of active rigs had increased by some 50% between 1978 and 1980.

From that starting point it stretched out three lines on a chart to illustrate three different possibilities (Figure 5):

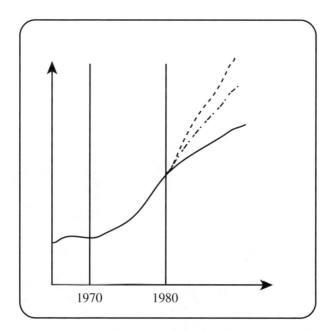

Figure 5   Three forecasts of the number of active rigs in the United States in 1990

+ an optimistic forecast;
+ a moderate forecast; and
+ a pessimistic forecast.

The pessimistic figures ran at some 25% below the optimistic
ones, and they were intended to take into account the worst
possible eventualities. The company then made its future plans
accordingly.

What happened in fact was that the market in new active oil
rigs in the United States completely collapsed after 1981 (Figure 6).

To the ill prepared, the collapse seemed to come like a bolt
out of the blue. Immediately before it, oil-related businesses had
been the darlings of the stock market. In the wake of the second
oil crisis, oil was considered a strategic resource and tax breaks
were being handed out by the American government in order to
encourage domestic drilling.

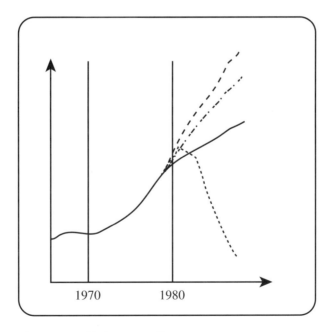

Figure 6   What actually happened!

But when President Reagan took over at the White House in 1980, he and his advisors considerably downplayed the strategic importance of oil. So much so that it was not long before the tax breaks to encourage domestic drilling were summarily removed. As a consequence, the actual number of active rigs in the United States in 1990 was less than one-fifth of the total number that had been predicted in the oil-equipment supplier's most pessimistic forecast. Needless to say, the company went bankrupt shortly after President Reagan changed the rules.

A string of examples like these further encouraged corporate planners to look for something that took them away from forecasting based on straightforward extrapolations from the past, and throughout the 1980s a growing number turned to scenario planning. There are still far too many corporations, however, whose corporate planning methodology is little more sophisticated than reading Tarot cards or sticking a wet finger in the air. Unfortunately, it often takes a severe shock to shake them out of their complacency. Even the Pentagon, for instance, only seriously considered the possibility of domestic terrorism in the United States after the Oklahoma bombing had shown how real that possibility was.

A new way of thinking

Scenario planning provides a framework in which to think about such possibilities; it gives a context in which to set seemingly random things that happen in the world. Suppose you pick up your newspaper in the morning and read that Harrods, London's top department store, has been bought by the Eagle Star insurance company. 'What an odd thing for Eagle Star to do,' you think, and pass on to the next item. 'With luck,' you say to yourself, '*The Economist* will tell me what it's all about at the end of the week.'

But if your company has done some scenario planning, such seemingly random events may well find a context in one of the scenarios that you have mapped out. It does not take too much imagination to come up with a future in which the retailing and financial services industries converge more and more. In such a context, an insurance company taking over a department store seems unexceptional. It can then be fitted into a wider context in which you have thought through all sorts of implications for your own business.

In the next five chapters of this book (Chapters 4–8) you will find some actual scenarios that have been devised by myself and a group of colleagues at Andersen Consulting. After reading them you will see that a take-over of Harrods by an insurance company would suggest that a scenario which we have called Keiretsu Rising (Chapter 5) is going to most closely reflect the real world.

One of the major problems with forecasting is that it encourages inertia. It looks for linear projections of the future and then asks for a fixed strategy that takes those projections into account. Once such a strategy has been chosen, and the necessary action taken to put it into effect, it is as if the corporation can cruise on auto-pilot until the next five- or ten-year plan is drawn up and a new strategic direction selected. The company behaves as if in the meanwhile it is going to meet no more solid obstacle than a puff of cloud, as if there are going to be no changes in markets or technology that are going to require it to readjust its strategy along the way.

Our way of looking at things, by contrast, encourages flexibility. Scenarios need constant care and attention; they have to be tweaked with every significant change in the environment. As Pierre Wack put it, 'Their purpose is to gather and transform information of strategic significance into fresh perceptions'. We have to be constantly alert in order to identify what new information is of strategic significance, and then we have to transform it into new perceptions.

Forecasts lock us into a particular view of the future, ideally a view that can be expressed in a small number of straight lines. It tries to take a still picture, a 'snapshot'. Our way of looking at things, on the other hand, presents us with a movie, a consistent but shifting picture of the world.

When electricity first appeared in domestic households it was largely used as a means for wealthy people to light up their dolls' houses. Forecasting the future of electricity then would have anticipated a market no more exciting than that for two-inch high wardrobes. A more flexible view of the future of electricity, however, would have evolved with the changing uses of electricity itself.

This whole approach to planning lays great emphasis on what are generally described as 'right-brain' functions. The two sides of the brain, left and right, are used for distinctly different purposes. The left-hand side is where the rational functions reside, our powers of reasoning and analysis; while on the right-hand side reside our intuitive abilities, those that lie 'beyond reason'. Forecasting depends primarily on the analytical skills that require the left side of our brain; our approach attempts to find a balance between both sides, between the rational and the intuitive.

The Canadian business academic Henry Mintzberg was one of the first people to argue that it is important for management to allow the right side of the brain to have equal sway with the left. 'The important policy-level processes required to manage an organisation,' he once wrote, 'rely to a considerable extent on the faculties identified with the brain's right hemisphere.' And certainly the processes involved in scenario planning as described by Pierre Wack—in his article in the *Harvard Business Review* quoted earlier—rely heavily on faculties that are generally identified with the right side of the brain.

Scenarios fit well into Mintzberg's view of the strategy-making process. In his schema, businesses start off with a strategic intent, a vision of what they want to be. But as time passes this gets buffeted about by forces in the external business environment, and the strategic intent has to be modified. The actual strategy which then emerges begins to veer away from the intended strategy with which the business began.

In this context, our scenarios can be seen as a way to narrow the gap between strategic intent and strategic reality. By drawing out scenarios that picture the effect of changes in the external environment, the planner can recognise early warning signals. He or she can then take action that will minimise the need for the organisation to shift from its original intended strategic direction.

Lock-in versus perpetual transition

At Global Business Network (GBN), the consultants illustrate the dangers of getting locked into one view of the world by means of an old map. Drawn by a cartographer called Herman Moll in 1701, it is a map of the United States, and many of its details are remarkably accurate. The Gulf of Mexico is more or less the right shape, and so are the Great Lakes.

But there is one very peculiar thing about the map, and that is the fact that it shows California as an island. The early cartographers of the area thought that the Gulf of California reached all the way up to San Francisco.

Widespread use of this map among European explorers had some unlikely consequences. There were, for instance, Spanish monks who landed at Monterrey and decided to haul their boats over the heights of the Sierra Nevada in order to relaunch them on the other side of what they thought was an 'island'. Their aim then was to sail across the straits to the American mainland.

When they found themselves (and their boats) on the edge of

the Nevada desert, the monks did two things. First, they abandoned their boats—leaving them to rot and providing future archaeologists with fodder for some far-fetched theories about the first settlers on the American continent. Secondly, they told the cartographers back in the Iberian peninsula that they had got it wrong.

Nobody, however, likes to be told that their maps are wrong, and that the myriad assumptions based on them have to be uprooted. And so for a long time the Spanish cartographers refused to believe the monks. Indeed, they found it so hard to undo their assumptions about the Californian coastline that they told the monks that they must be looking in the wrong direction!

And so for many years sailors floated around California with a totally false mental map of the area. At best, this map was misleading; at worst it was downright dangerous. Likewise, businesses which find their way around their markets based on maps made by forecasters (with an early eighteenth-century sense of their own infallibility) are in danger of having a totally false mental map of the area in which they operate. IBM at the beginning of the 1980s was just such a company. Its mental map of the computer industry contained all sorts of islands which Big Blue failed to see were all part of one contiguous continent.

Planning in today's business world

The unavoidable fact of the matter is that the business world today is in a state of perpetual transition, a transition that is taking place ever more rapidly. Forecasting survived for as long as it did because it was being used in a world where change took place at a less frenetic pace. Managers today need new tools to cope with this qualitative difference in their environment, and to enable them to spot significant changes quickly and to understand their significance.

Such is the nature and intensity of the change that is taking place that we believe it marks nothing less than a shift from one economic era to another. Not surprisingly, a shift of such magnitude requires a new type of economic model to describe it. Just as the industrial revolution marked a shift from an agrarian economy to an industrial economy, a move from the farm to the factory, so the technological revolution is bringing about a shift from an industrial economy to an electronic economy, a move from the factory to the computer-based workstation. At Andersen Consulting we call this the eEconomy. Electronic technology permeates every single aspect of the economy today. It goes way beyond eCommerce.

At the moment we are in the midst of the transition from one economy to another. We don't know how long that transition will last, but while it continues it creates a very difficult business environment. It is an environment in which old certainties have been undermined and new ones have not yet been formed to replace them.

There are, however, a number of things that we can say about the eEconomy with a reasonable degree of certainty. It is, for example, a global economy, because electronic communications and the Internet acknowledge no geographical boundaries. It is also an economy in which organisations are structured in new ways—ways that break free of the military models inherited by the early management experts on organisational structure. Companies today are organised in a more democratic way: e-mail and other forms of electronic communication genuinely do 'empower' employees by giving them the knowledge and information that is needed for them to make decisions. Knowledge, not labour or capital, is the main asset that is driving business today.

The relationships between organisations and individuals in this new economy are very different from what they were in the industrial economy. In the industrial economy relationships were either totally binding and designed to last for ever—lifetime employment contracts, for example, or corporate take-overs, where one company absorbed another, forever. Or they were so loose and informal that they could be abandoned at a moment's notice—suppliers for example, or casual labour.

In the eEconomy relationships will be very different. There are many more of them and new ones are being formed on an ad hoc basis all the time. By and large, they are very task-oriented, formed in order to achieve a particular objective, with the idea that they will be disbanded when that objective has been reached. They are neither casual nor eternal—a new order of things that was well reflected by the images of schools of fish in Andersen Consulting's pioneering television advertisements.

This transition is putting firms in a double bind. Not only is it making it more difficult for them to take a view of the future, it is also making it more urgent that they do in fact do so. Never has the need for a new approach to planning been so acute.

Using the tool

Over the years, the process of drawing up scenarios has been standardised to some extent. But you should always bear in mind that you want, at the end of the exercise, to be left with a number of scenarios that achieve at least three things:

1 they focus on issues of importance to your business;
2 they tell stories which are distinct, different and memorable; and
3 they don't tell stories about things which are already known with a reasonable degree of certainty.

The first step is to find somewhere to start, and this is best done by focusing on one essential issue, on something that is of particular concern to your business. It may be something very general, such as the impact of new technology, or of new competitors. Or it may be something more specific, such as the impact of the parlous state of the Japanese economy.

NIER, a Japanese financial consultancy, undertook the latter sort of exercise, and it began by asking more than 100 people in Asia, Europe and North America what they thought would be the course followed by Japan over the next 20 years. Out of these discussions the consultancy extracted three scenarios.

One was essentially pessimistic, reflecting the fears of many people that Japan would not be able to make the structural changes to its economy that were deemed necessary to avoid financial collapse. The second scenario was more optimistic, reflecting a situation in which major reforms began to take place which, in their turn, spurred further reforms in what soon became a virtuous circle. The third scenario focused on a single issue which the participants in the process had brought out as being possibly of great significance: the withdrawal of America's military presence in the Far East and its effect on enforced Japanese neutrality.

The three scenarios were each given names to reflect their different character: 'The long hollowing'; 'Crash and rebirth'; and 'Hercules departs', respectively.

In the scenarios that I sketch out in Chapters 4–8 our focal issue is the interplay between consumer-serving industries and consumers. We chose this focal issue because we could see major changes taking place and wanted to know 'where they might end up'.

And we drew out scenarios that reflected this issue at its extremes. There is no point in painting scenarios where you know that the differences between them are going to be too subtle for you to be able to draw out any useful insights. For instance, don't try to map out two different scenarios such that in one there is an assumption that average annual GNP growth between now and the year 2005 will be 2.5%, and in the other there is the assumption that it will be 3.5%. Indistinguishable scenarios are not going to stick in anyone's mind. And, above all, you want your scenarios to make a distinct impression on the minds of your employees. So home in on issues that are guaranteed to grab their attention. New acquisitions, for example, or relocating the headquarters.

Once a focal issue has been identified, go on to list the key factors which influence that issue—the changing nature of consumer demand, for instance, or competition, present and future. Trying to decide whether to launch a new direction in R&D would focus discussion sharply on the relevant science and technology. A focus on capital investment would involve looking at financial markets and the way in which they are evolving.

The next step is to identify those things in the general environment which have the most powerful effect on these factors. What things are going to have most influence on the development of financial markets, for instance? Government regulation? Or private pension provision? And what new science is going to have most impact on your core product? Nanotechnology? Or the invention of new materials?

Getting answers to these questions is vital to the whole process. And you will only get good answers if you have drawn together the right group of people with access to the right information. That means the people best able to see the significance of today's changing circumstances for your organisation.

By this stage, the group needs to have drawn up two lists: on one are the key factors influencing the focal issue that was identified at the very beginning of the process, and on the other are the outside environmental forces that have the most powerful affect on these factors. The group should then try to rank these lists according to their importance, and also in their order of uncertainty.

The point of this particular part of the exercise is to find the two or three things that the group agrees are the most influential and also the most uncertain. Having identified them, they then become the axes in a one-, two- or three-dimensional diagram (Figure 7).

This diagram defines what scenario planners call the 'logics' of the different scenarios that are going to be drawn. Peter Schwartz describes these logics as being, 'The plot which ties together the elements of the system'. They are, if you like, the bare bones that the planner then sets about 'fleshing out'.

We created two axes which initially gave birth to four different scenarios. The axes can be seen as stretching from east to west and from north to south. The east–west axis reflects different

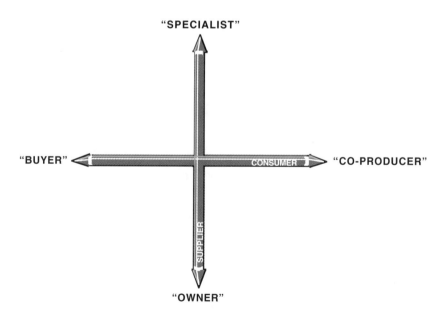

Figure 7   The logics of different scenarios

types of consumption. In the west we have a world in which consumers buy ready-made products—baked beans, washing powder, etc.; in the east, consumers buy tailor-made goods, from bespoke suits to customised computer games.

The north–south axis reflects different styles of production. In the north we have a world of specialists where firms are narrowly focused on satisfying needs across a narrow band of the value chain. In this world, in order to satisfy customers firms have to form alliances with other specialists. In the south, producers attempt to 'own' for themselves a stake in all the links in the value chain.

Our scenarios then draw out the extremes of these axes taken in combination. One is at the extreme north-east corner, the second is in the south-east corner, the third, in the south-west, and the fourth in the north-west. Taking the extremes in this way helps to emphasise the differences between the scenarios. It also reinforces the point that the whole process is not about making predictions, but about thinking of possibilities.

The possibility of there being a fifth scenario, a wild card that could not be fitted into this structure, was built into our thinking from the beginning. And at the end we considered it to be such a possibility that we described it as a separate scenario.

Once you have drawn the bare bones of the scenarios in this way, you are ready to flesh them out. To do this, take each in turn and consider all the key factors relevant to it one by one. And then try to describe where they might take you.

At this stage it is important not to forget the other environmental forces and uncertainties that were listed in the early stages of the exercise, but which did not come high enough to have been shortlisted. Make sure that they feature somewhere in the stories too, and that you take time to consider their implications.

Once the scenarios have been painted, turn your attention

back to your focal issue and see how it looks in each of them. If you had chosen, say, the issue of whether to make a major acquisition in a new industry, and it looks like a sound decision under all the scenarios, then what are you waiting for? If it looks good in only a few, identify where the risks are most likely to arise, and consider what you can do to reduce them.

Part of the value of scenarios lies in their ability to bring order to what might otherwise appear as a series of patternless incidents. Within a scenario, such incidents may come to be seen as early warning signals, indicators that one particular story is more likely to unfold than any other.

In many cases, early warning signs indicate movement along only one particular axis, not necessarily towards a specific scenario. For instance, in our work any event signalling the failure of synergistic business partnerships might suggest that specialists are going to find it more difficult to thrive in future. It would not, however, necessarily say anything about the nature of consumer demand.

Signs that suppliers are becoming more specialist might include:

+ a general growth of open standards;
+ a growing number of collaborations among companies proving to be genuinely to the benefit of all of them;
+ the emergence of a number of successful value-chain specialists.

Signs that suppliers were moving along the axis in the direction of 'owners' might include:

+ little agreement on international standards;
+ synergistic partnerships failing and giving way to mergers and acquisitions;
+ delivery channels remaining proprietary.

If consumers were moving in the 'buyer' direction along the horizontal axis, we might expect to find that:

✦ industry's attempts to sell products based on an underlying need was being met with tepid enthusiasm;
✦ consumers still making purchase decisions based primarily around price rather than fit;
✦ corporate revenues were continuing to come from the selling of 'traditional' products.

If consumers were moving in the opposite direction, becoming co-producers with suppliers, we might expect to find that:

✦ organisations were beginning to acquire personnel or skills from outside their own industry;
✦ products and services based on satisfying consumers' needs were overwhelmingly popular with a very time-conscious public;
✦ vendors selling non-traditional products suddenly became very successful.

Action-oriented organisations might want to draw up lists of things that they think they should do (or should not do) as a consequence of the scenario planning exercise. These things can usefully be divided into three:

1 The 'no-brainer' items—those things which make sense whichever scenario pans out, and which should therefore be implemented regardless.
2 The 'no-gainer' items—those things which make no sense in any scenario, and which should therefore be avoided at all costs; and
3 The 'no regrets' items—those things that are beneficial in some scenarios, but which are not life-threatening in any.

Firms also need to set down systematically the implications of the early warning signals that they have identified. Any signs of protectionism creeping back into national legislation, for example, should set alarm bells ringing and point the planners down a particular path. The implications for their business of following that path should be clearly spelt out, and should include a list of things that firms can do in order to benefit most from the evolving environment.

Finally, firms should draw up a list of the general areas that they need to think about each time that they are reviewing or revising their scenarios. The list is almost bound to include things like the regulatory environment, changes in consumer behaviour, and new developments in information technology. It should also include a number of things that are more specific to the individual firm.

The process at Andersen Consulting

Our process began with my getting a small group of industry experts together to consider the possible structure of the consumer-serving industries in the future. With the help of our Center for Strategic Technology Research (CSTaR), based in Chicago, the group began by seeking to answer two specific questions: 'How will industries respond to changing consumer needs, and how will industries be driving these needs?'

Our group included people with high-level knowledge of IT-intensive businesses such as retailing, financial services, utilities, government and transportation. We had experts from all parts of the globe, and in particular made a point of consulting people sceptical to the whole idea, people wedded to tradition, and others who could roughly be described as 'free thinkers'. There was also an attempt made to consult people from all age groups.

Out of this discussion process the group drew up a list of all the main forces that it was felt would have a bearing on the answer. And the top two forces on the list were:

1   *The role of the supplier in the value chain.* Can we expect companies of the future to be categorised according to the things that they produce, or by where they operate in some broader value-creating network? This, in turn, broke down into three sub-issues:
    —Will companies in the future maintain their position on the value chain?
    —Will they attempt to reach further up (or down) it? Or
    —Will they try to reduce their position and make it even narrower?

2   *The role of the consumer.* Will consumers want to choose from a multitude of predefined products or will they seek to co-design and/or co-produce things that satisfy their needs? Do they want to be buyers (largely as they are today) making price-based purchasing decisions, or do they want to be co-producers making value-based purchasing decisions based on finding solutions to their specific problems?

When plotted along two perpendicular axes these forces gave us our four different scenarios. Together with the fifth scenario, the wild card, these scenarios are described in detail in the next five chapters.

Each chapter is written as if it were already the year 2008, and each begins with a general description of the business environment at that time. Within that description, the chapters focus on what each scenario means for the consumer, for suppliers and for the marketplace.

The chapters also consider what some of today's major companies might be doing under the different circumstances. This is meant to highlight those differences by setting them in a specific context, and the companies have been specially chosen for that purpose.

In one scenario, for example, we foresee the Ford Motor Company focusing on its core competence to such an extent that it does nothing else but assemble automobiles; in another scenario we see Ford competing with Walt Disney in the theme park business—as well as assembling automobiles.

We have also given each of the scenarios catchy names because we believe it is important to be able to attribute anything that seems like an early warning signal to one scenario or another as quickly as possible. And it is far easier to do that if you have to recall the nature of something called Keiretsu Rising than of something called Owner/co-producer, or K2.

Our scenarios

We called our five scenarios Sun Chasing; Keiretsu Rising; Acme & Co; Excelliance; and Thunderstrike (Figure 8).

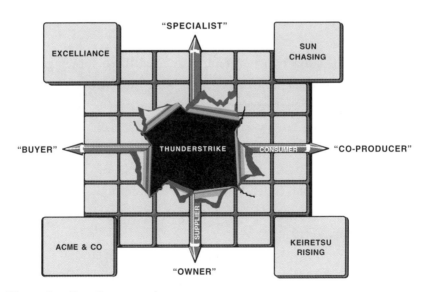

Figure 8   Our five scenarios

In **Sun Chasing** the world economy is booming. Suppliers are highly specialised, and they make their goods and services in co-operation with consumers who add their own specifications in order to meet their particular needs. It is a world where only the nimble survive. Demanding consumers flit from one supplier to another, and suppliers are constantly changing the narrow range of products that they supply.

The industrial scene is characterised by global specialists, and the dividing lines between industries have become blurred. Open technologies and global regulations have reduced the barriers to entry in all markets, and new entrants are frequently to be found locked in battle with traditional industry suppliers.

Keiretsu Rising is also characterised by co-producing consumers, but this time they exist in combination with huge networks of firms which straddle value chains from one end to the other. Firms within the same network come together in order to meet an individual consumer's needs, and each network tries hard to satisfy all its customers' demands. (*Keiretsu* is a Japanese word meaning something like 'headless combine', a good description of how these organisations work.)

The *keiretsu* have been nourished by an environment in which there is a proliferation of competing standards and regulations. These, in turn, have been encouraged by a widespread growth in nationalism and regional protectionism.

In **Acme & Co** owner/producers are combined with the type of consumer who wants a wide range of products to choose from, but doesn't want to be involved in the creation of those products. This is a scenario in which the old-established firms of the twentieth century fight back against the technology-inspired newcomers of the twenty-first century. By merging into ever-bigger units they eventually force their way to the front through the sheer vastness of their scale. This is a scenario where brawn beats brain.

Consumers base their purchasing decisions almost exclusively on price. Price is the overwhelming driver of markets, and customer loyalty is something that is rarely seen. The vast conglomerates produce goods and services that are almost indistinguishable from one another. Winning corporations in this world have to be masters of re-engineering and of cost reduction (not just of cost control).

At the fourth extreme on the chart stands **Excelliance**, a combination of the words 'excellence' and 'alliance'. Here firms excel at one tiny segment of the value chain, and in alliance with other specialists they produce standard products and services for a marketplace where regulation and technical standards are harmonised to a remarkable degree. In this scenario, consumers have totally forgotten that variety was once said to be the spice of life.

Winning firms in this scenario are truly excellent at their core skill and at working together with their alliance partners.

Finally, in our fifth scenario, **Thunderstrike,** all these neat classifications fall apart. The world economy is on its knees after an extended period of conflict across many parts of the world, and war is right now spreading throughout Asia. An ultra-nationalist government has recently taken over in Russia.

Populations which have been strafed with war, poverty and fear for extended periods of time are in no mood to lead a consumer boom. All across the world the 'consumer' has all but disappeared, to be replaced by something that looks more like a 'survivor'. Companies too can do little more than hope to survive as they search to find a role for themselves.

To come

These are just five scenarios. Remember that there are countless more besides these five that we could have devised based on other significant forces. And remember too that each one of them (those that we have described and those that we haven't) will to some extent reflect future reality.

On the other hand, it goes without saying that the real world is not going to ape any one of our scenarios precisely. In practice it is going to be an amalgam of all of them. Some might feature more strongly in one part of the industrial environment than in another. So, while one scenario might seem particularly true for one segment of the population, a second scenario might seem more applicable to another. The huge mergers that took place in the commoditised financial services industry in the United States in mid-1998 suggested strongly that the Acme & Co scenario was unfolding. Yet in other industries—such as media and software—the alliances among narrow specialists that were taking place at much the same time seemed to suggest that Excelliance was the most likely scenario of the future.

But whatever the early warning signals are suggesting today is the future for your industry over the next ten years, you can be sure that they will flash quite contradictory signals on a number of occasions between now and 2008.

Chapter summary

In this chapter I look at a way of planning that can help organisations look to the future. It is based on a tool called scenario planning, which is described as being 'designed to help companies and the people who work in them to take a longer-term view of their business in a world of increasingly rapid and unpredictable change'.

Scenario planning involves bringing people together so that they can paint a number of possible pictures of the future, and can then draw out the implications for their organisation. It is used by a growing number of the world's largest corporations—among them Royal Dutch/Shell which was largely responsible for its early development. The Anglo–Dutch oil company's more successful strategic response to the OPEC-induced oil-price hikes of the 1970s is widely attributed to its early introduction of scenarios.

The chapter looks at the traditional alternative to scenarios—straightforward forecasting where the future is drawn as an extrapolation from the past. But extrapolating along straight lines based on past experience has proved to be a poor guide throughout most of history. The chapter includes a number of colourful examples.

The world is full of uncertainties, and discontinuities are the norm. Continuity is the exception, but we were lulled into a false sense of security by the continuous and steady growth of most major economies in the first 30 years after the Second World War. The oil price hikes of the 1970s were the first major economic discontinuities in the second half of the twentieth century, and they brought home to corporate planners the need for new tools to help them make decisions about the future.

The result is to traditional forecasting as the movie camera is to the still photograph. Traditional forecasting attempted to build a structure, a corporate plan, which would last unchanged for five or ten years. The planning that we are looking at, by contrast, is a continuous process that allows organisations to move forward while taking into account the perpetual change that is the norm in today's business world.

The chapter goes on to describe the process of making scenarios, drawing on the work of one of the world's leading scenario planners, Global Business Network (GBN), and a book, *The Art of the Long View*, written by GBN's president Peter Schwartz. It explains the way in which we drew up our scenarios, the essential steps in that process, and the bare bones of the pictures that began to emerge. Those pictures are painted more fully in the following five chapters of the book.

2008

4

Sun Chasing

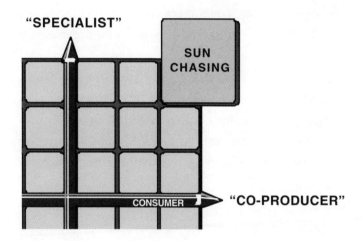

IN THE TOP RIGHT-HAND SQUARE OF OUR TWO-BY-TWO MATRIX IS
the specialist/co-producer scenario. This we have called Sun
Chasing. It is a scenario in which in the year 2008 the world
economy is booming. Rates of growth of GDP in Europe and
America have been at historic highs for several years. Countries
such as Spain and Canada have experienced annual growth rates
in double figures.

All the events predicted in this book are educated guesses about what might happen in the
business world over the next decade, written from the historical perspective of the year
2008 as though those events had already happened. It is not intended that any reader
should place any reliance whatsoever on any prediction or other statement made in this
book. The author and publisher of this book disclaim any responsibility whatsoever for any
consequences of such reliance.

But some of the most dramatic growth rates are occurring in what were once called 'emerging markets'. Nations such as Russia and Thailand now enjoy standards of living comparable to those of western Europe in the late 1980s. More relaxed regulation and the development of high bandwidth communications technology have been largely responsible for jolting these emerging markets into the mainstream world economy.

The world of Sun Chasing is one in which highly specialised producers come together with consumers to customise products and services for them. The latest red-hot computer game, for instance, is invariably produced by a small company in Taiwan or the Czech Republic. Such a company then supplies the whole world with a basic platform for the game. The platform consists of some highly sophisticated graphics which only the manufacturer can produce, but customers are able to add on many features of their own, features which have been agreed with the manufacturer at the time of ordering.

The combination of a high degree of specialisation with the globalisation of markets has been encouraged by widespread deregulation and technological advance, and these have also helped to establish new ways of working. Today's employees are freed from many of the old constraints of time and place. Most people work when they want, and where they want (which frequently means at home). This freedom has increased productivity and helped to push unemployment rates to an all-time low.

The massive lay-offs of the 1990s ultimately proved to be a transitional phenomenon. Industrial historians now see them as a symptom of the painful shift from one commercial era to another—from the industrial economy to the electronic economy. The electronic economy in which business is conducted today is an economy of full employment.

The globalisation of markets has been accelerated by recent

advances in high-speed logistics. A new generation of cargo jets that can cross the Pacific non-stop at speeds above the speed of sound has brought America very much closer to the markets of Asia, and vice versa. The planes are a little bigger than the old Boeing 'jumbo' jets, and they fly at speeds close to those of the old Concorde passenger planes. In addition, new design features in the planes have made them so extremely efficient in the use of fuel that air-freight rates across the Pacific have halved in real terms over the past ten years.

In parallel to this there have been great advances in marine transport. Huge container-carrying catamarans designed and built in Scandinavia have halved the journey time between European ports and the east coast ports of America. Just as the Internet has given consumers the capacity to shop simultaneously at hundreds of different electronic 'malls', transport systems have evolved that enable those malls to deliver goods to customers anywhere, and at a low cost.

The globalisation of both suppliers and consumers has made the world a much smaller place. For instance, when trade between Europe and Asia was opened up with the EAAPP (Europe and Asia Preferred Partner agreement) in 1999, many regional products from both Europe and Asia were introduced into each other's respective markets for the first time. Initially, suppliers had expected that their products would appeal only to expatriates living in the regions—to Europeans in Guangzhou and Singapore, for instance, or to Asians in Dusseldorf and Glasgow.

The greater openness of consumers to foreign products and services has stimulated a wave of entrepreneurialism, especially in the countries of the European Union. Creative individuals and investment Euros (the Union's ten-year-old single currency) have been highly successful in searching for new fishing grounds in the ocean of global opportunities. They have discovered that in the world of Sun Chasing, new entrants can compete in most markets just as effectively as old veterans.

The increased movement of goods around the world has been matched by mass migrations of people, encouraged to move by the more relaxed attitude of most governments to immigration. Greater freedom to travel and to pass information across borders has helped to reduce tension between nations.

Global communities of like-minded specialists have bonded together in a way that ignores their place of birth, their hometown or their religion. These communities of specialists keep in touch electronically, and they have regular 'get-togethers' via cheap video-conferencing links.

Many groups have been thrown together electronically by the similarity of their purchasing patterns rather than of their specialist skills. The Internet is a place where like tends to seek out like. There is, for example, the World-wide Association of Quake Enthusiasts. Known as 'Quakers', they collect and disseminate on-line information about the world's oldest computer game called Quake. Via the association, players are able to find new ways to customise their product—for example, to add new levels and characters to their original purchase.

As long ago as the late 1990s, leading organisations began to realise that fundamental changes in consumer behaviour were going to demand new ways in which to fulfil consumers' needs. And for the past five years or so companies have lost interest in marketing to specific geographic areas. Instead they push their products and services to electronically linked communities such as the Quakers.

This has forced companies to radically rethink the ways in which they do business. They now find that they have to focus sharply on one specific core competence and to put all their energies into being 'best of breed' at that particular point on the value chain. The Swiss company Nestlé, for instance, no longer makes chocolate. It has evolved into being the world's leading supplier of cocoa paste, and it counts all the major chocolate manufacturers among its clients.

The consumer

In the Sun Chasing scenario, consumers are intimately involved in producing goods and services to satisfy their needs. This new pro-active relationship between consumers and producers has given rise to a new expression for consumers: they are now widely referred to as 'prosumers', pro-active consumers who take part in designing and producing the products that they want.

Information technology has alerted prosumers to the fact that there is now a vast number of global suppliers eager to satisfy their individual needs. In 1955, for instance, there were on average three varieties of shampoo available to the average consumer in the UK. By 1995 that number had risen to 75, and today it is nearer 1,000.

Consumers realise that they are no longer obliged to accept the standard products offered by suppliers. There are now dozens of groups of specialists happy to collaborate in order to provide customers with personalised products. The customer who wants a personalised shampoo, for instance, can feed into the Internet the details of the colour, age, length and texture of their hair and of the environment in which they spend most of their time. The supplier groups then come together to concoct a suitable product for that customer and bid for the business.

Consumers now put their demands out into the marketplace and wait for them to be met. This is a reversal of their former modus operandi, in which suppliers put their products and services out into the market and then waited to see if they met consumers' demand.

Generation Xers, people born in Europe and North America between 1965 and 1981, have become the main engine of consumer demand. The 'Baby Boomers', the generation that preceded them, are now for the most part highly active retirees.

Generation Xers were the first generation to learn how to use computers in their childhood. Using the Internet to gain access to all sorts of services is therefore something that they have taken to with ease. The parent at home today is not washing dishes and ironing while the children are at school. He or she is more likely to be studying for an on-line degree or running a Web-based business that only makes calls upon their time when the children don't. 'Home workers' like this typically work in shifts with other specialists so that they can adjust their working hours to fit in with the rest of their life.

The penetration of the Internet into almost every household has revolutionised many industries. The way in which cars are bought, for example, has changed radically since the 1990s. In the early years of the electronic age, consumers used the Internet to browse around looking for the lowest prices. They then used that information solely in order to negotiate a better deal with their traditional car salesman, who worked through a traditional dealership.

This squeezed the profits of car dealers very rapidly and put many of them out of business. The average net profit to a dealer on the sale of a new car in the United States fell from $600 in 1990 to $200 in 2000.

Nowadays consumers wanting to buy a new car use an Automotive Search Agent. After entering their requirements—for example, a Jaguar chassis with a Porsche-designed turbo-charged engine, a wood-panelled interior and an Alpine sound system—they wait to receive an offer.

A purchaser who recently asked for a Jaguar chassis with a Porsche engine received six proposals within the space of a couple of hours. Two of the offers were close to what he was asking for, while four of them met his requirements precisely. The four varied slightly, however, on price, and the customer eventually selected one that was provided by an organisation called Cayman Automotive. He was swayed by the fact that it had a number of attractive tax advantages.

The speed at which offers for cars come through depends a bit on the time of year. In many countries the main time for buying new cars is just after employees have received their holiday bonuses, and this has a visible effect on the speed at which information and orders are processed.

The markets

Markets these days are very open. They are characterised by the free flow of vast quantities of knowledge and data from company to company and from customer to company. Consumers would be overwhelmed by information were it not for the fact that there are large numbers of intermediaries prepared to help them sort out the information and to focus on what is relevant to their needs.

Regulation, long seen as a barrier to entry into markets by newcomers, has been all but eliminated, and markets are now largely self-regulating. The vast quantities of data flowing in the public domain make markets and the organisations that operate in them largely transparent to the consumer. Consumers are encouraged to look out for themselves instead of relying on quasi-governmental agencies or private-sector vigilantes to watch out for them. The old phrase 'caveat emptor' ('let the buyer beware') would be essential today were it not for the fact that competition is so intense that suppliers bend over backwards to avoid upsetting their customers.

Government's role in industry and commerce has been largely 'hands off' for some years now. And this applies to governments from all shades of the political spectrum. An American Democrat, President Bill Clinton, set the ball rolling with his 'Less Government' initiative at the end of the last century. The European Union and governments in other western nations soon followed suit; today most countries leave industrial policy to be moulded by experts drawn from industry. The inability of political leaders to keep up with rapid changes in technology and its implications for business has been the downfall of at least one administration, and has caused severe headaches for many more.

The EU has been a strong proponent of the laissez-faire attitude to governing industry, and it now concentrates its energies on encouraging competition and on protecting European interests elsewhere in the world.

It has, for example, been particularly active in protecting the use of trademarks and of brand names belonging to European luxury goods manufacturers. The luxury fashion and accessory business is now almost totally concentrated in Europe, built on the tradition begun in the last century by legendary French and Italian designers such as Yves St Laurent and Gianni Versace. But there is no shortage of eCowboys offering allegedly 'original European designer goods' which customers discover (after they have been delivered) are no such thing.

The EU actively pursues any electronic cowboy brought to its attention, and it is deeply involved in formulating new legislation and new international agreements that make fraudulent copying more difficult. But the fraudsters are as nimble as any successful entrepreneur, and no sooner has one new market or technical loophole been blocked than they find another.

The reduced amount of political intervention in industrial policy has proved popular with the general public. Voters believe that it has given governments more time to carry out what they maintain should be their chief role in society today—the design and fulfilment of programmes that further international relations and social welfare.

Many national governments argue that although their role in industry is less direct, it is no less influential. They say that it is an individual country's education, welfare and other social programmes that ensure that its industry has the workforce that it needs. And those programmes are still the responsibility of government.

Furthermore, maintaining good international relations is vitally important to the conduct of business today. Goods and services are produced by partnerships of specialists who often live in a number of different countries. When one of those countries has a disagreement with the international community it can have widespread repercussions.

Take the case of Albanian marble. The very best marble today is almost all polished and finished in Albania. Imported from Italy, the raw stone is transformed by craftsmen who have a skill that cannot be found anywhere else in the world. From Tokyo to Toronto, the lobbies of the most luxurious hotels and offices are today furbished with Albanian marble.

A few years ago, however, an Albanian minority government attempted to force all its Muslim citizens to convert to Christianity. After months of international pressure failed to persuade the government to change its mind, the United Nations imposed a blockade on the tiny European nation.

This had an almost immediate impact on the world market for marble flooring. The price rocketed and a lively second-hand market for finished marble grew up. Ancient sites around Europe and the Middle East were plundered for their marble, and world concern at this development was instrumental in persuading the United Nations to remove the Albanian blockade a few months after it had begun.

In many cases, governments work with private-sector companies and their specialist networks to ensure that good international relations are maintained. The Albanian government was persuaded to drop its proposed legislation on compulsory conversion by the marble workers themselves. They were in electronic contact with marble buyers around the world who informed them of attempts to revive marble-polishing skills in places like Sicily and Georgia, a revival that would have threatened their future livelihood.

Despite their laissez-faire attitude, governments retain the right to introduce new legislation pertaining to industry at any time. The only significant act passed by the EU in recent years, however, is one that was designed to ensure that certain environmental guarantees are met. It gives the EU powers to fine firms heavily if they fail to meet declared targets for the reduction of pollution. Most EU business leaders see occasional 'feel good' legislation like this as the price they must pay if they wish to continue to have a relatively free hand in their own affairs.

In general, though, markets are open, and getting more so. This is being helped by the virtually universal standardisation of technology which is allowing newcomers to enter all sorts of technology-driven businesses relatively cheaply and quickly. The availability of low-cost unlimited bandwidths also helps by making possible the transmission of vast quantities of data to consumers who, thanks to the development of interactive media, sit in the comfort of their own homes while maintaining direct two-way contact with suppliers from all over the world.

Industry's perspective

Traditional dividing lines between industries have become blurred because organisations now focus on becoming world class at one particular point on the value chain. The idea of there being things like 'banks' and 'automobile manufacturers' which take responsibility for the whole chain has almost totally disappeared.

Banking services and cars are now supplied by groups of specialist organisations that come together in a fluid way to meet individuals' specific demands.

The ability of firms to compete on the basis of a fairly narrow core competence has allowed once struggling companies from the former communist bloc and from third-world nations to become major players in global markets. So much business now takes place 'over the wire' that geographic location is rarely an issue.

Within this framework there are specialist intermediaries that aggregate individual components of the value chain in order to come up with customised products and services that satisfy prosumers' demands. Called 'value chain integrators', these agents both anticipate prosumers' demands in advance, and also respond to them retrospectively.

Industry is characterised by these narrowly focused global specialists. And they rely heavily on advanced networking technology and on their efficiency at their core competence for their survival. Alliances of these specialists come together and then break apart depending on customer need. Firms can find they are partners on one job and competitors on the next. Electronic links that have bound them together one day may have to be untangled the next.

This has led to the development of sophisticated programs that allow small parts of a network to be continually unwound and then rebuilt as the alliances of those with access to the network change.

There are no longer single firms that make all the bits that go into a washing machine, for example. Customers wanting to buy a machine ask a value chain integrator to put together whatever combination of features they require. The integrator then turns to the specialists that it thinks are best able to meet the customer's needs.

This has stopped the wasteful practice that used to occur in the past when washing-machine owners would use only a small fraction of the number of programmes that their machine was built to perform. Nowadays there is no reason to have a machine that does anything more than its owner requires.

The continuing deregulation of industries around the globe and the development of new enabling technologies have lowered the barriers to entry at many points along the value chain. This has had a big impact, particularly in industries such as financial services where tight regulation in many countries had for years severely restricted the number of new entrants into businesses such as banking or stockbroking.

In the United States, repeal of the Glass-Steagall Act a couple of years ago removed one of the last remaining barriers to banking in that country. The Act, passed as long ago as 1933, had prevented commercial banks from underwriting or dealing in securities for almost three-quarters of a century. It was finally repealed because underwriting and dealing in securities had become such an open business that commercial banks were almost the only institutions that were still prevented in some way from taking part in it.

The Glass-Steagall Act had been passed originally for some perfectly good reasons. A number of scandals had exposed banks using depositors' money to support the price of securities that they were underwriting. But the danger of such a situation recurring after the repeal of the legislation was thought to be small. Massive flows of information now pass between companies and consumers, and there are many search agents on the World Wide Web that analyse information about those who provide financial services. It is easy for consumers to tap into this information.

Anybody who wants to make a deposit can find out very quickly what are the credit ratings that a number of these agencies have given to various deposit-taking institutions. They can also find out some of the measurable levels of risk to which the institutions are exposed.

Some leading companies today

The unfolding of the Sun Chasing scenario has required all leading companies to make major changes in the way that they operate and in the businesses that they operate in. They have had to decide on which part of the value chain they wish to place themselves, or whether they want to be value chain integrators. In the space of only a decade some of the world's biggest and most successful firms have been completely transformed.

For example, in the late 1990s the very successful Finnish mobile-phone company Nokia felt the pressure of shrinking margins and global competition, and it decided to sell off most of its operations. The result is that Nokia is now a renowned research and development business. The retooled company, called Nokia Research, makes no direct sales to consumers; it prospers largely by making technological breakthroughs in wireless communications, data-storage techniques and the use of blue-laser technology.

The company sold its mobile-phone manufacturing operations to Compaq, which at the time was an American computer manufacturer in a business that was increasingly becoming commoditised. By buying Nokia's mobile-phone operations, Compaq signalled a sharp change in strategic direction. For the American company had decided to become a specialist manufacturer of hardware 'shells', basic boxes to which others supply software. Compaq now produces computers for companies such as Microsoft, which then gives them away free to customers who buy its software.

Likewise, Compaq manufactures mobile-phone equipment for telecoms service providers all over the world. Many of these are given away by the service providers as part of a package that ties their customers for some time to their particular services.

Quite recently Compaq bought the car-manufacturing operations of the Japanese firm Mitsubishi. This it is going to develop in much the same way as it has its computer and mobile-phone businesses. The customers for its Mitsubishi cars will be the growing number of service providers to the automobile industry—suppliers of satellite traffic-monitoring devices, audio systems, and car video-phones, for example. None of these firms is yet giving cars away free in return for a customer's commitment to their services. But a number of analysts expect that such a day is not far off.

The Ford Motor Company has also gone through a dramatic transformation. In the late 1990s it realised that a fundamental change was taking place in its market. Rapid economic growth in the west meant that its customers there were becoming more and more discerning. They were no longer content with the standardised 'world cars' that Ford had pioneered—one model that with a few modifications could be sold anywhere in the world.

Customers wanted differentiated personalised cars, and this went against the trend of the industry. Compelled by a desperate need to cut costs, it had been gradually reducing choice by limiting the number and variety of models that it put on the market. Something had to give, and in the end it was not the consumer.

While the demand for more personalised products was growing in the west, markets in India and Southeast Asia were exploding. Demand for cars there grew particularly rapidly, even though in many of these countries the car is more of a status symbol than a means of transport. The density of population is such that many roads are dangerously congested.

Stories abound of commuters in cities such as Bangkok and Bombay taking seven or eight hours to travel the few miles between their offices and their homes. Commuters who want to travel more quickly stick to the bicycles that their forefathers used. The very wealthy buzz around in helicopters, and the skies above some of these cities are now in danger of becoming dangerously congested.

Trying to be a complete car manufacturer in markets such as these made Ford realise that it was stretching itself too thin. It decided that it needed to focus more narrowly if it was to be a viable link in the value chain for an industry that had become truly global and highly customised.

So in 2002 the company went through a massive restructuring. It sold off its non-core manufacturing businesses, getting rid of all its designers, all its component-manufacturing bits, and all its (vast) lending business. What was left was a streamlined world-class automobile manufacturer with flexible links to a large number of companies around the globe.

Ford now uses these links to deliver customised cars to consumers in all its markets. For instance, it often works with the Porsche Automotive Design group, the organisation that bought Ford's own design business in 2002. And it frequently uses Honda engines in its cars. The Japanese company which (like Ford) used to be a fully integrated car manufacturer is now a maker of engines, and of nothing else. It went through a major restructuring at about the same time as Ford, and it saw much the same strategic options for its future. Honda's engines now power everything from lawnmowers to helicopters.

Barclays' Square

Twenty years ago Barclays was one of the UK's biggest banks, and there was scarcely a high street in the land that did not contain one of its branches. Today, however, Barclays is a completely different type of operation. Most of its business is carried out

electronically, and virtually the only property that it owns is a leafy
'campus' in the highlands of Scotland.

The change in Barclays' business began in the late 1990s
when its Internet-based financial services began to take over from
its branch-based business. The bank closed more and more
branches and laid off more and more staff as it came to focus
increasingly on electronic services.

The success of these on-line services was enough to persuade
Barclays to expand into other areas of electronic shopping. It set
up a new organisation to broaden its range of on-line shopping
services, and it called it Barclays' Square.

By the turn of the century Barclays' Square was running a
number of virtual shopping malls on the Internet. In practice, all
the company provided was a channel of communication together
with an intuitive interface that enabled 'shoppers' to navigate the
channel. But the service quickly proved to be more profitable for
the Barclays organisation than its traditional financial services
businesses.

Spurred on by a catchy advertising slogan ('e buy Barclays'
spoken in a north of England accent), the company went from
strength to strength. It now owns 17 on-line malls and takes a
percentage of every transaction that is carried out on them. But
Barclays never actually takes possession of any of the things that
are sold. That is left to the networks of suppliers who use the
malls in order to market their products.

Each of the 17 malls on Barclays' Square caters to a different
community of interests. There is, for example, the Garden Mall
where amateur and professional gardeners can buy plants and
gardening equipment from every corner of the world. The mall
also provides customers with crucial advice on the sort of climate
and soil that different plants require.

One of the Garden Mall's most successful services is tailored
to meet the needs of people who are moving into a new house. In

today's flexible global economy people move home more frequently than they used to. If they want a new garden to go with their new home, all they need to do today is to give the Garden Mall their precise address. From its database it is able to tell for most locations the quality of the soil and the nature of the climate.

Based on that information it can then draw plans of different landscaped gardens, taking into account any requirements specified by the customer—if, for example, they want a pink garden, or a Japanese-style garden, or a garden within a certain budget. Customers then choose the plan they prefer, and the materials needed to make such a garden are sent directly to them. If they want someone to do the hard labour, that too can be provided.

So successful have the malls become for Barclays that the company has just changed the name of its overall umbrella organisation to that of its on-line services business, Barclays' Square.

BG Plc

Another company whose business has been radically altered by the ubiquity of the Internet is British Gas. Until late last century it was the monopoly supplier of natural gas to British homes. But then the company was privatised, and its monopoly market was opened up to competition.

This had two effects in particular: first, it narrowed the company's profit margins considerably, and secondly, it forced the company to think of new ways to keep its shareholders happy.

This rethinking led the company's directors to decide in 2001 that they should focus their business on its most valuable asset: direct contact with almost every home in Britain. So British Gas completely restructured itself, gave itself a new name (BG), and set about becoming a one-stop shop for catalogue services.

Although the growth of eCommerce was phenomenal in the early years of this century, direct selling via catalogues and the telephone continued to grow rapidly as well. Today there are more electronic catalogues than printed ones, but many customers still like to talk over the phone with trained staff before they make an electronic purchase.

BG's seven-days-a-week, 24-hours-a-day call centres have some of the most highly trained customer service representatives of any organisation anywhere. Even though the call centre operatives live all over the world and rarely get to meet each other, they provide a consistency of service which customers find appealing. They frequently win plaudits in consumer polls.

BG now services a very wide range of catalogues selling everything from banking to soft furnishings. The company also, incidentally, occasionally finds itself taking an order from a customer for the delivery of some natural gas.

British Telecom and British Integration Services

British Telecom's story is rather different. In the late twentieth century it was one of the biggest and most profitable companies in Europe. After having been sold off to the private sector, it had managed to develop its business in the fast-growing telecoms market very successfully.

By the late 1980s, however, the company had begun to realise that it could not remain dependent on its relatively small domestic market in the UK. So it devised a grand strategy designed to turn it into a truly global supplier of telecoms services.

But the strategy suffered from a series of setbacks. A proposed link-up with the American telecoms company MCI fell through unexpectedly, and approaches to major telecoms operators in Germany and China were inexplicably rebuffed.

Not only did BT find itself overly dependent on its domestic market, but it also found itself in a market that had become a prime target for a host of new entrants into the telecoms business. These companies, many of which came from abroad, set about cherry picking BT's business in the UK. And they were soon able to make big inroads into a number of markets that BT had traditionally considered its own.

The company then set about a number of highly publicised 'corporate reorganisations'. But these only made incremental improvements to its results, and they had adverse long-term effects because the company handled the massive lay-offs that were involved very badly. It got rid of its youngest and newest recruits first, and then found itself left with a group of long-serving elderly senior managers who were unable to seize the opportunities presented by fast-changing telecoms technology.

By 2002 the company was deeply divided. The older generation of employees continued to resist change while a bunch of younger executives in the services division were pushing hard for the chance to move into new markets. In particular, they had their eye on the markets for telecom and systems integration services.

After a long and acrimonious battle, the company was finally split up into two business units: one continued to be called British Telecom, and it provided more or less the same services as the company had always done, selling access to the telecoms network that the company owns, maintains and updates; the other was called BIS (British Integration Services), and it began to offer some of the multitude of new services which a network like that owned by British Telecom is able to supply. It was not long before BIS outgrew the parent that gave birth to it, and last year its turnover was three times that of British Telecom.

What it takes to be successful

To succeed in the Sun Chasing world, organisations have, first and foremost, to be nimble and able to respond quickly to new market demands. Accurate market research is valued very highly today. Certain research firms are known for their ability to identify changing patterns in consumer behaviour at an early stage. Like other businesses, the market research business has itself become very specialised. There are firms that watch nothing but the behaviour of particular generations.

Some of the most successful businesses today consist of networks of specialists who live in countries and time zones far removed from each other. This enables all of them to work at hours that suit each one of them while at the same time providing the sort of 24-hour a day 'We Never Close' type of service that is expected of today's global organisations.

A common pattern is to find a partner in Australia looking after the business while colleagues in Europe sleep. The Europeans then hand over to partners in the United States who keep the business going until Australia takes over again. This pattern builds teams that have a broad multi-cultural outlook at the same time as they have a narrow focus on their core abilities, an essential combination for success in today's world.

Firms also need to be able to respond rapidly to changes in market demands, and their responsiveness has to be measured in terms not only of their ability to innovate but also in terms of their ability to integrate new technologies and business processes into their own organisation, as and when appropriate.

Workers have to learn new skills and techniques continually, and they have to adapt their working life to take these on board. This often means that parents have to change their working hours at short notice, a task that is made easier by a new flexibility in schools.

So much education today takes place over the Internet that children spend more time doing 'home work' (i.e., work at home) than they do at school. Moreover, the modules that they do need to complete at school can be done at times that suit them. The power of the consumer and the demand for convenience have made a big impact on the market for education.

Early warning signs

With the benefit of hindsight it is possible to see a number of industrial trends that at the time (and for those who were able to see them) acted as early warning signs of things to come. Three in particular are worth mentioning:

1 There was a gradual acceleration in the number of new entrants into a wide range of businesses. Newspapers were full of stories about firms that had suddenly decided to start something completely different and gone into a business that a few years earlier would have seemed (for them) most inappropriate.

   At the same time a large number of companies were leaving businesses which had seemed to be at the very core of their existence a few years earlier. The case of British Gas getting out of gas was one; the day that Nokia produced its last mobile phone was another.

2 A second signal came from the size of the new entrants into a range of industries that had traditionally been the preserve of very large firms. Nothing seemed too big for a little newcomer. This led to a whole host of David vs. Goliath stories in the pages of the business press.

   Laker, Virgin and others started the ball rolling when they took on the airline giants in the 1980s. Virgin subsequently decided to run a railway and an insurance company as well, both of them operated as virtual organisations. Nowadays this type of industry structure is so common that it is hard to remember how original it seemed at the time when Virgin was first spreading its wings.

3 Finally, it should have been possible to foresee the Sun Chasing scenario evolving from the sort of alliances that companies were forming with each other. In the first enthusiasm for alliances and joint ventures, companies went into them as if they were to last forever. And even when they brought them to an end, it was with regret and with a feeling that their ending was an indication of some sort of failure.

Only gradually did companies come to realise that alliances were made to be broken, and that they necessarily had a finite shelf life, lasting only until their specific purpose was attained. But once this idea dawned, companies rapidly adjusted their behaviour, making and breaking alliances at short notice. Short-term, task-oriented inter-company alliances soon became the key to business success in all areas. This new sort of temporary link became known as a dalliance, a combination of the words 'alliance' and 'dilly-dally'.

Chapter summary

In the Sun Chasing scenario, the world economy is booming. Rates of growth in Europe and America are at historic highs, and some of the most dramatic growth rates are occurring in what were once called 'emerging markets'. More relaxed regulation and the development of high bandwidth communications technology have jolted these emerging markets into the mainstream world economy.

In the Sun Chasing scenario the consumer is king. Now called prosumers, they invite global companies to satisfy their individual needs. They are highly demanding, and they only establish relationships with suppliers that deliver value. The spread of information has made them fully aware of the range of choice that is available to them from a multitude of suppliers.

Markets are very open these days. They are characterised by the free flow of vast quantities of data from company to company and from customer to company. Consumers would be overwhelmed by information were it not for the large number of intermediaries that help them to sort it and to focus on what is relevant to their needs.

Regulation, long seen as a barrier to entry into markets by newcomers, has been all but eliminated, and markets are now largely self-regulating.

Globalisation and technological advances have been the main forces shaping the industrial scene. So much business now takes place 'over the wire' that geographic location is rarely an issue.

The dividing lines between industries have become so blurred that traditional industry categories have ceased to exist. Industry is now characterised by narrowly focused global specialists which rely heavily on advanced networking technology and their efficiency as their core competence. Alliances of these specialists come together and then break apart depending on customer need.

Within this framework there are some new types of organisations. For instance, there are things called 'value chain integrators' which aggregate individual components of the value chain in order to come up with customised products and services that satisfy the demands of today's consumers.

Many of the world's most famous firms would be unrecognisable to a Rip Van Winkle who had been asleep for the past ten years. The Ford Motor Company has become a narrowly focused world-class car assembler with flexible links to a large number of companies around the globe. It restructured itself dramatically six years ago, shedding all its non-core manufacturing businesses.

Barclays Bank has become the owner of 17 on-line malls and has changed its name to reflect its new main business. Nowadays it is called Barclays' Square. The former British Gas is called BG and is a major catalogue sales channel. British Telecom makes three times as much money from new services that it offers over its network as it does from the network itself.

To be successful in this environment companies need, first and foremost, to be nimble and able to respond quickly to new market demands. Some of the most successful businesses today consist of networks of specialists who live in countries and time zones far removed from each other. This enables all of them to offer the sort of 24-hour a day 'We Never Close' type of service that is expected of today's global organisations.

Finally I recognise three developments at the turn of the century that were, as it now transpires, early warning signs of things to come. There was the rapid escalation in the number of new entrants into industries across the spectrum; there was the fact that a growing number of these new entrants were small firms; and there was the growth in the number of short-term alliances between companies, alliances that were formed for a specific purpose and which were then disbanded when that purpose was successfully achieved.

In Chapter Five I go on to look at a very different scenario.

5

Keiretsu Rising

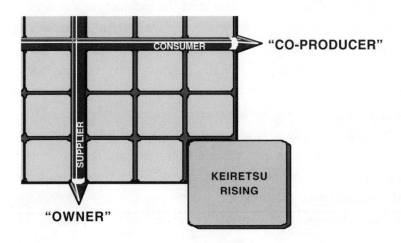

"CO-PRODUCER"

KEIRETSU RISING

"OWNER"

Iɴ ᴛʜᴇ ʙᴏᴛᴛᴏᴍ ʀɪɢʜᴛ-ʜᴀɴᴅ ᴘᴀɴᴇ ᴏғ ᴛʜᴇ ᴡɪɴᴅᴏᴡ ғᴏʀᴍᴇᴅ ʙʏ our two-by-two matrix is the owner/co-producer scenario. This we have called Keiretsu Rising.

Keiretsu is a Japanese word meaning, literally, 'headless combine' and it is the name given to a form of Japanese corporate structure which came to be widely admired in Europe and the United States in the 1990s. A seminal article in the *Harvard*

Business Review of July 1996 described how the American car company Chrysler had created 'an American keiretsu', and this was followed by popularisation of the idea in the general business press.

Virgin's chairman, Richard Branson, compared his company to a keiretsu. 'At the centre of our keiretsu brand,' he wrote in late 1996, 'will be a global airline and city-centre Megastores acting like flagships for the brand around the world.'

This was followed by an article in the influential *New Yorker* magazine in October 1997 in which the American keiretsu was described as 'the next corporate order'. At about the same time, an American-style keiretsu called Cendant was enjoying great success on the stock market—its share price grew by 2,000% in the five years after its flotation in 1992. Investors loved the company, which embraced businesses such as Ramada Inns, the Avis car-rental business and the NCP car parks. Despite a brief troubled period when the accounts at one of its businesses were called into question, the company went on to become a model for the predominant form of corporate structure in most parts of the world.

In the original Japanese version of the keiretsu a number of independently managed companies owned small stakes in each other and worked together in a variety of ways. This enabled them to supply customers with a range of products and services that, in the case of Mitsubishi, stretched from bank accounts to air-conditioning systems.

This web-like structure was adapted to suit different business cultures in different parts of the world so that today, in 2008, all large organisations are essentially made up of vast networks of small manufacturers and service providers which have pledged to co-operate with each other in order to meet consumers' demands. The networks are held together by extremely sophisticated information systems, and the range of services that the big keiretsu offer today is even wider than that offered by their Japanese predecessors in the 1990s.

The economy

The world in which these keiretsu operate is one that is starkly polarised between the very wealthy and the very poor. The gap between the haves and the have-nots has widened dramatically over the past 15 years.

The gap is not so much between people of different nations as between different groups within nations. The beggars in Paris and London, for example, are today much like those in Calcutta and Djakarta; the life of the wealthy successful businessman in Bombay is little different from that of his counterpart in New York.

All over the world the wealthy live in ghettos, apartment blocks that are ringed with security guards and defensive walls. Beyond the walls are the poorer sections of society, people who for the most part live on the streets. Inside the ghettos people have access to highly sophisticated communication systems, and they make great use of these in order to avoid having to go outside and having to face how the other half lives.

These communication systems are capable of delivering sophisticated interactive educational programmes directly into the homes of the 'haves'. Most countries today have a better-educated workforce than ever before, albeit a workforce that represents a smaller percentage of their population than ever before.

While Spain, for example, has an unemployment rate of over 25%, it also manages to send some 30% of its young people to university. One part of the explanation for this peculiarity is that the children of the haves, no longer crazy about going out to play on the streets, have little better to do than to watch interactive educational TV.

The high levels of education have given birth to a new breed of educated consumer who knows what he or she wants and who is articulate enough to explain those wants to suppliers. In many cases customers are intimately involved with suppliers in creating their own purchases, and this has inevitably brought suppliers much closer to their customers.

Anybody today who wants to make a purchase, even of something as insignificant as, say, a vase, gets in touch with a keiretsu and is presented with a number of choices. The keiretsu might first ask what substance the customer would like the vase to be made of—glass, ceramic, metal, or whatever. They might then discuss the size; is it for a single flower, or for tall bunches, or what?

At this stage the customer might say that they want it to be made of a design of their own specification. Alternatively, the keiretsu might show to the customer (via the Internet or via interactive television) a number of different designs that it has created, and from which the customer might prefer to choose.

Payment is organised electronically, and the customer is encouraged to use a payment system that belongs to the same keiretsu as the vase maker. Using any other payment system is bound to be more expensive.

The keiretsu then arranges for the product to be delivered to the customer's address. Most dwellings these days have secure delivery 'boxes' where everything from the weekly groceries to a bunch of red roses can be dropped off by the armoured delivery vans that are the most conspicuous feature on the roads of most cities. Many of these delivery boxes have special refrigerated compartments where foodstuffs can be left. Access to the boxes is gained through the use of a unique pin number that the customer quotes when first ordering goods from the keiretsu.

The demanding nature of consumers has been instrumental in forming the large conglomerates that dominate the industrial world today. The need to offer highly tailored services that continually meet the evolving needs of individual customers has forced organisations to get together in a way that enables them to encompass an enormous breadth of skills.

Most of these organisations, however, have developed along regional lines, and regional affiliations, both at the political and economic level, are stronger today than they have ever been.

There are, for example, keiretsu that are clearly identifiable as American, and there are keiretsu that are clearly identifiable as European. Part of the explanation given for this lies in the fact that organisations within a keiretsu are frequently called upon to work together at very short notice. And firms have found that this is easier if they have similar cultural backgrounds. They don't then have to spend valuable time discovering the social taboos of others working on their team.

The conglomerates leap geographical boundaries wherever there are cultural similarities. Hence many Spanish companies work within South American-based keiretsu, and Anglo-Saxon keiretsu frequently link organisations from North America, the UK and Australia.

This means that industry itself is less global than many people once expected. Japanese companies have withdrawn from their manufacturing plants in Europe and America, and almost all the joint ventures that once existed between Chinese and American firms have been disbanded.

Consumers, however, are ensuring that markets retain some semblance of being global. Ford automobiles are in demand all over the world, and so are Benetton clothes and Scotch whisky. Consumers want fast personalised service, and they don't mind where it comes from. If a foreign keiretsu can meet their needs at a good price, they will use it.

But politicians, in general, conspire against globalisation. They are lobbied aggressively by the big conglomerates which attempt to persuade them to put the interests of their regional keiretsu before all else. In many cases they are successful. Many regional governments, for example, have been persuaded to adopt the local keiretu's proprietary systems as industry standards.

Interestingly enough, many politicians believe that this has occurred largely as a reaction to what was seen as American dominance of the software industry at the end of the last century. At that time several newly emerging keiretsu outside America began promoting their own proprietary technologies without waiting for international standards to emerge. This led to considerable divergence in the standards used by industries in different parts of the world. For instance, it is no longer possible to buy a PC in the United States that has a built-in ability to access the Internet from Europe.

The abandonment of many of the attempts at international standardisation has left conglomerates free to develop their own unique delivery channels and novel value-added services. These proprietary systems continue to be a key way in which the keiretsu gain competitive advantage over their rivals. Customers today do not want to sign up with a large number of interactive electronic 'shops'. So they carefully choose the smallest number that seems able to meet all their needs.

Once a consumer is hooked into one or two keiretsus it is extremely difficult for them to shift. If they do attempt to end a relationship, they are immediately bombarded with special offers and highly persuasive sales talk by the keiretsu that they are trying to abandon.

Many customers, of course, threaten to leave a keiretsu merely to see what it might offer them to stay. But the keiretsu design their systems in a way that maximises the cost to customers of transferring to a rival.

The region in which the keiretsu have grown most markedly has been Europe. There they have been encouraged by the growing cultural homogeneity of the area and by the industrial structure of the individual countries.

In the late twentieth century many of the member states of the European Union (EU) had national 'champions' in a number of industries. While these firms were often big in their domestic markets, they were frequently too small to compete in the global market, or even in an enlarged regional market. So since the late 1990s the European Union has been encouraging the formation of keiretsu-style alliances between some of the biggest of these national champions.

This strategy has been highly successful. The EU's scattered bunch of national industry champions have come together in a way that now seems almost like a process of natural evolution.

Once they realised that they needed help to meet the diverse demands of global consumers, firms formed many different types of alliance with each other. Some of these links tied together firms in the same industry; others were formed by firms in completely different industries. The electrical giant Phillips, for example, is at the heart of a keiretsu which embraces firms from almost every industry and from every member country of the EU. The Barclays Group sells everything from Renault's cars to Electrolux's washing machines.

The alliances often helped individual firms to overcome their reluctance to enter new markets. The barriers to entry in many areas have risen sharply with the failure to agree on international standardisation, and many firms recoil from the cost of entering new markets on their own. When they are integrated into a major keiretsu's network, however, the cost of market entry falls sharply.

Many firms say that they got together in order to meet the demands of the marketplace better. But at least as compelling a reason for a large number of them was the threat from new entrants. By the end of the last century small nimble newcomers were able to go 'cherry picking' in many of the big established corporations' most lucrative markets. In telecoms and banking, for example, markets that were being revolutionised by developments in information technology (IT), small firms were able to make big inroads by offering cost-based pricing on a limited range of services.

The new entrants carefully chose services that the big players had been using for years to cross-subsidise other bits of their operations. Thus, for example, the percentage (by value) of trans-Atlantic telephone calls handled by the big national telecoms champions of Europe fell from 100% of such calls in 1990 to less than 5% in 2000.

Such actions inevitably provoked radical reactions. For many, the first reaction was to seek shelter under the umbrella of a large keiretsu. Most of Europe's smaller national telecoms companies, for example, have come together and used economies of scale to fight back against the cut-price tactics of the small operators. They have also done everything they can to persuade the EU to let them have the European market to themselves.

The consumer's perspective

In the world of Keiretsu Rising, consumers define the products that they want and then ask the big conglomerates to come up with ways in which they can be produced. This applies to cars as well as to meals.

Consumers know what they want; and they want it now. Successful keiretsu have developed systems that enable them to deliver goods and services as and when they are required. These days any sort of cuisine can be delivered to most urban homes within 20 minutes of an on-line order being given; a request to see a Frank Sinatra cabaret show from the early 1950s, for example, can be met almost immediately by one of the many entertainment channels; and a customer who says 'I feel like lying on a Balinese-style beach this afternoon' may well be able to do just that at a local leisure centre. If they are lucky, it will be a day when the centre has a special offer on Balinese breaks, complete with virtual sea, sun and sand.

It is unfortunately much more difficult for a consumer to get to Bali itself. The poverty and unrest mean that the only safe way for tourists to reach their destinations is by helicopter. They are whisked away from the high security airport where their supersonic jet lands, and from there they are dropped directly onto the helipad of their resort hotel. They are then unable to leave the hotel compound (which is inevitably surrounded by high banks of barbed wire) until it is time for their return—when a helicopter takes them straight back to the airport.

There are few opportunities for tourists to go shopping while they are on trips like this. Partly this is because they simply don't want to. They know they can find almost everything that the world has to offer without straying far from the safety of their own residential complex.

There are a number of ways today in which consumers go shopping. Depending on their wishes and the product, they buy things either from branches of the big keiretsu or over the Internet. Most keiretsu have representative offices on the malls that are found attached to the sheltered apartment blocks of the wealthy. The malls are full of keiretsu's offices, and they look as dull as a British building society in the 1990s. Most of them consist of rows of computers manned by service agents.

The agents' job is to help customers to design their own products. A young executive looking for an anniversary present for her parents, for example, would go down to her local mall in the evening after dinner and call in at the office of the Barclays' Group. The agent there would have no difficulty showing a range of washing machines—the gift that the executive had in mind—

because the Electrolux company has an exclusive distribution arrangement with Barclays.

The executive will receive a discount if she uses her Barclays Visa card to make the purchase, and she will receive bonus points (known as 'Barclays' bucks') in proportion to the price of her purchase. These she can set against the price of any merchandise that she buys from the Barclays Group in future.

Consumers who are merely making repeat purchases, buying something (like the weekly groceries) that they have bought many times before, prefer to use the Internet. Research shows that 85% of Americans and 75% of Europeans use the Net for repeat purchases.

However, when customers are looking for a solution to a particular need (like the executive who wants to buy an anniversary present for her parents) they usually go into a representative office. There they can discuss their options with a service agent at the same time as they refine what they want via direct on-line contact with a potential supplier.

There is always a single point of contact for customers within every keiretsu. Although consumers' demands can usually be met only by putting together a large number of components produced by many different organisations, it is always the keiretsu itself which takes overall responsibility for delivering the solution to the customer's needs. Customers' complaints about faulty goods are not made directly to the particular concern responsible for the goods.

That means that when customers have a faulty product there is a single organisation to which they can complain. It is not like the old days when firms would toss the responsibility from one to another. Today, all organisations within the keiretsu realise that one bad apple can make the whole barrel rotten. They are as keen as the customer to find out where the fault lies and to make sure that it is corrected.

On occasions there have been disagreements between

organisations within the same keiretsu as to where responsibility lies. But on such occasions a senior member of the conglomerate acts as arbitrator and allocates responsibility speedily. All organisations have to agree to be bound by such arbitration procedures before they are accepted into the group. Taking industrial disputes to law is widely recognised as being too slow to meet the needs of today's consumers.

In the marketplace

The key to markets today lies in knowledge and information. Successful groups invariably have highly sophisticated systems that allow data to flow fluidly and rapidly both across and between companies that are 'members' of the same group. The rapid dissemination of information within groups allows members to come together in a unique way in order to serve one individual customer, and then to come together in a slightly different way in order to serve the next.

Andersen Consulting has itself been a pioneer of such systems. In the late 1990s it built up what it called a 'Knowledge Exchange', a system that used Lotus Notes software to bring together the collective intelligence of the firm's 60,000 consultants. This in itself was a massive change from the days not too long before when the organisation had relied on a single manual to distribute its collective knowledge.

A total of over 2,000 databases are today continuously updated with information that the firm's consultants gather in their day-to-day work. As the keiretsu around Andersen Consulting has grown, the Knowledge Exchange has also grown.

It is a feature of today's markets that firms are created and dismantled at a far faster rate than in the past. For many years now, the major economies have been reporting large increases in both the number of new companies being registered and the number of old ones being liquidated. What's more, the rate of increase in those numbers is still accelerating.

It has become essential therefore that keiretsu be flexible enough to take on board a constant flow of newcomers at the same time as they discard those companies whose natural life has come to an end. This they have to do without endangering the security of the system. So they have to be sure that firms leaving the group (for whatever reason) are not going to take proprietary information with them and sell it to rivals—or merely broadcast it anonymously over the Internet.

Because of the central role of knowledge and information in the competitive battle between different groups, there have been a number of landmark legal cases trying to establish who 'owns' knowledge. But despite the millions of dollars that these cases have cost, the law is still not entirely clear on the matter. In the meanwhile, conglomerates watch very carefully to see that members of their group do not use what they consider to be the group's 'knowledge' as if it were their own.

A key technology in marketing the goods and services produced by the keiretsu is the high bandwidth on-line facilities that carry information in and out of customers' homes. For most consumers the 'point-of-sale' is an electronic terminal, which means that they buy products without actually being able to touch them. So they want to get as good an electronic 'view' of those products as possible on their terminals.

Keiretsu therefore compete fiercely on the quality of their proprietary on-line services, repeatedly making new claims about their customers' ability to see things in three dimensions and in their 'true' colours.

The regulation of markets today is in general very light. After extensive lobbying by big industry over a number of years, the EU, for one, changed its attitude quite dramatically. It now allows business for the most part to take the lead in setting industrial policy.

Anti-trust legislation dating from the last century is still on the statute books in many countries, but it is widely ignored. And even when it is not ignored, the law is based on such old-fashioned concepts of ownership and control that groups today can side-step it quite easily by structuring themselves carefully and taking the advice of a good lawyer. For instance, it is rare today for any one company within a keiretsu to 'control' any other company within the group. The implications of control can be quite oppressive.

Nevertheless, many of today's conglomerates are of such size and scope that opponents of these concentrations of industrial power (and there are some very vocal opponents) argue that they would not have held up to the scrutiny of anti-trust authorities six or seven years ago.

Many small firms struggling to enter new markets have argued that this new industrial order has been created at their expense. 'Small', they say, 'is not beautiful any more.' Or at least 'small and isolated' is not beautiful. As a small firm within the tentacles of a large conglomerate it is possible to be highly successful, but rarely otherwise. Most new ventures seek first to be embraced by one of the big keiretsu before they ever bring a product or service to market.

Small firms claim that new barriers to entry into various markets are prepared almost daily by bureaucrats in Brussels and elsewhere. Far from being 'hands-off', they say, the regulators are as busy and interfering as they ever were.

By and large, however, the complaints of small firms and other anti-monopolists fall on deaf ears. Although the system is widely acknowledged to be hard on new entrants that want to remain independent, consumers are so much in favour of it that it has been impossible to persuade any judge for a number of years that individual cases of industrial concentration are against the public interest.

In essence, the EU does everything it can to help companies from within its borders to join with other firms from within the EU. It then tries to encourage these groups to market themselves all over the world. More or less the same formula is followed by governments everywhere. The world economy today is far less dynamic than it was ten years ago.

Industry's perspective

The keiretsu conglomerates themselves are highly diversified. The range of their output changes over time, based on shifts in consumer demand, but each keiretsu aims to be able to satisfy the needs of most of its customers most of the time. The sheer size of the groups means that it is rarely necessary for them to reach outside themselves in order to meet a customer's needs.

The keiretsu structure has developed largely because it gives customers a single 'shop front' from which to purchase their customised products. It is many years now since Benetton, an Italian clothing company, realised that it could customise the colour of its garments much more easily if it enlisted the help of another firm to do the dyeing for it. That principle is the driving force behind today's industrial structure.

The need for speed is generated by the nature of today's consumers and their rapidly changing tastes. The keiretsu try to maintain close relationships with their customers in order to keep up with these changes. To help them, firms have developed sophisticated in-house systems that capture highly detailed information about their customers. These track their purchasing patterns, and it is easy nowadays for a firm to know when each individual customer needs, say, more heating fuel or a new packet of cornflakes.

The conglomerates are sharply focused on trying to 'own' customers, and they compete fiercely in their attempts to lock consumers into their particular group and its range of products and services. Groups are continually reinforcing the bond between customer and supplier by encouraging two-way communication.

The way in which industry attempts to lock customers into a single supplier is reminiscent of certain businesses in the twentieth century. Customers then were also often locked into a single supplier (like IBM in its heyday, for instance) because they were committed to its standards and could find them nowhere else. It was too expensive for them to switch suppliers, and in those days it was often too difficult to find the information on which to base a decision to switch.

To some extent things have gone full circle. After an era of open systems, firms have once more chosen to design their own proprietary systems and distribution channels. It is again expensive and time-consuming for consumers to find out what competitors are offering. So, once again, they tend to stick with suppliers who are familiar to them.

This has put a high premium on brands, and most of the keiretsu are fronted by powerful brand names. Ford, Barclays, Disney and Virgin are some of the best-known brands in the world today, and behind each of these names lies a wide range of products and services. It is beholden on all firms operating within each of these keiretsu to maintain the good name of the overall brand since part of its value belongs to them.

A keiretsu will go to great lengths to strengthen the loyalty of customers to their particular brand. Many of them have developed sophisticated customer loyalty programmes that encourage people to continue buying from them. As I have already mentioned, Barclays and its partners offer what they call 'Barclays bucks'.

All these offers are equivalent to 'frequent buyer' points and are gained in proportion to the amount spent on goods and services from firms within the group. Points can be credited against the price of any products or services purchased from other firms within the keiretsu.

Some groups' bonus points have become almost like a national currency. Many travellers, for example, find it easier and cheaper to use their points when they are abroad in order to avoid having to make expensive conversions from one national currency to another.

One EU resident wrote recently to *Business Traveller* magazine to say that he had spent a whole week travelling around Mexico without having had to spend a single unit of the local currency. He had 'spent' points from the Shell keiretsu to buy all his petrol and groceries (from the supermarkets that are now found on the forecourt of most Shell petrol stations), and he had used Barclays' bucks to pay his hotel bills (at the Amex-Continental) and to hire a car (from Eurohire).

As the major groups come to offer more and more similar ranges of products and delivery options, exceptional quality of service and the effective utilisation of an intimate and ongoing knowledge of customer preferences, interests and objectives become critical differentiators between firms. Groups spend a great deal of time and money on developing new ways to analyse and (more importantly) to anticipate shifts in consumer behaviour. This begins with demographics, but nowadays is greatly influenced by new thinking about people's 'mindsets', the frame of mind in which customers approach the buying experience.

From computer analysis of the purchasing patterns of individuals, companies can find out not only what time of day a person is most likely to make an expensive purchase, but also to what extent abstinence from purchasing is likely to affect their response to, say, an advertisement.

Since advertisements are now despatched to individual TV-

PCs, companies can time their advertising with great precision. For example, advertisements for luxury goods like boxes of chocolates are often targeted at those households above a certain income level that have not made a purchase above a given sum for more than a given number of days. Such people are particularly receptive to any temptation to 'spoil' themselves.

Advertising (both on-line and by more traditional means) has grown enormously in recent years. The new development in the industry is interactive advertising via television. Suppliers put forward their proposals for new products and services to consumers, and consumers respond by adding their own suggestions, all of it done on-line.

Many of the suggestions, of course, are mutually incompatible, so suppliers have to choose between them. But this sort of advance market research is essential today for companies that want to be in a position to supply products and services as and when they are required.

What famous companies are doing

A number of companies that were prominent at the end of the last century have changed their spots quite surprisingly in recent years. The Finnish company Nokia, for example, was a market leader in mobile telecoms for the best part of a decade. But a few years ago competition from Asian manufacturers forced it to think long and hard about how it could maintain its market share.

In the end the company decided to build up closer relationships with those firms that it deemed from past experience to be 'best of breed' suppliers. Gradually these firms clustered closer and closer around Nokia until eventually, as a group, they introduced a joint on-line marketing service which they called NokiaNet.

Consumers who interact with NokiaNet can now do

everything from co-designing with Nokia their next customised telecommunications product to purchasing durable goods made and sold by other companies in the Nokia consortium. A large number of manufacturers other than Nokia can today be accessed via NokiaNet.

The Ford Motor Company, arguably the twentieth century's single most successful firm, is set fair to win that title in the twenty-first century. It has become the market leader in tailor-made transport, manufacturing everything from bicycles to tanks to meet individual customers' specifications.

The company's durability has been truly remarkable. Not only did it remain one of the world's leading automobile manufacturers for more than 70 years, but it has also thrived during the past decade, a time when seven out of 1999's top ten car manufacturers have disappeared from the face of the corporate world.

The company gained its current competitive edge by being the first to offer customers a service whereby they were able to have a direct input into the way that their Ford vehicle was designed and manufactured. Ford discovered before most that by working very closely with a large number of tightly knit suppliers it could produce customised automobiles in a matter of days. Some of those vehicles are almost wholly assembled at the plants of Ford's component suppliers; the more standard products are largely put together in Ford plants. The result has been unprecedented demand for Ford vehicles, and for other products from within the Ford keiretsu.

At first, customers made their requests by means of a network of Ford kiosks that were linked directly with the company's own production control centre, or via the Internet. In recent years, however, customers have increasingly been using interactive television to buy cars. They have been enticed by newly developed technology that allows them to take vehicles for an 'interactive test drive'.

The Barclays' Group has followed a more unlikely route to success. It built on its early experience with Cars Direct, a car sales operation that grew out of a search in the early 1990s for ways of adding value to the group's personal loan business. Once the bank (as it then was) realised that it could turn an old commodity product like personal loans into a higher margin service by also selling the things that its loans were being used to purchase, there was no stopping it. Soon it was selling houses to go with its mortgages and package tours to go with its foreign exchange . . . not to mention a load of household appliances such as washing machines and cookers.

By the end of the last century, Barclays was a supplier of a vast range of goods and services which it sold directly to consumers through its network of branches. Buyers were offered substantial discounts if they purchased Barclays products using one of Barclays' own payment systems—be it an on-line payment, a card-based payment, or a good old-fashioned cheque.

The discounts (and faith in the Barclays' brand name) proved to be sufficient to bring customers flocking to what had once been a local bank in order to buy everything from food mixers to bedroom suites. Today the Barclays' Group embraces such a wide range of businesses that its annual profits from traditional financial services are less than a half of its profits from its other businesses.

An almost equally dramatic transformation has taken place at British Gas. In the early 1990s British Gas was a dull utility whose operations were largely confined to supplying gas within the borders of the United Kingdom. It was, however, unexpectedly offered the opportunity to set up a number of partnerships with American firms such as Union-Pacific Railway and Pacific Telesis.

These partnerships enabled British Gas to spread its wings into the building and maintenance of a number of large infrastructure projects in other countries. And these proved so successful that the company set about methodically establishing foreign partnerships all over the world. Nowadays it frequently finds itself competing for work with a similar large group that has formed around British Petroleum, itself once just an oil-exploration and oil-refining business.

British Gas's greatest success so far has been the winning of the contract—in partnership with a number of other international and local firms—for the provision and maintenance of most of the natural gas pipelines to the cities of Bombay and Shanghai. Its ability to handle these mega-projects has given the group an enviable reputation among national and local governments in the developing world, so much so that a majority of the group's revenues now come from the world's poorer nations.

British Gas is now a rare example of a company whose nationality has not yet been a deterrent to doing business abroad. Despite frequent discussions in the boardroom about how it is no longer British, and no longer exclusively involved with gas, the company has perversely chosen to stick with its name.

British Telecom's story has been of a business that has failed to fulfil the promise that it showed at the end of the last century. It has retained the word British in its name because its market is still essentially in Britain. In the 1990s a number of opportunities to forge partnerships with companies in the United States and continental Europe were missed.

By the end of the century the company found that many of its markets were being stolen from under its nose by nimble newcomers, and it came under severe pressure to split up into two separate business units. This was against the grain at a time when most businesses were getting closer together and forming networks of partnerships among themselves.

The reasons given for the split when it happened (in 2000) had more to do with the need for flexibility than with any hope of improving profitability. Customer demands were changing so fast even then that firms were realising that they needed to become more agile in order to keep up.

The firm's two business units (now called British Telecom and British Integration Services) have not split as far apart as top management suggested at the time that they might. As part of the same keiretsu they still find themselves frequently working together to meet specific customer demands.

British Integration Services focuses exclusively on providing telecoms services, but these are tightly integrated with British Telecom's high bandwidth network. Essentially the two companies team up to offer a host of integrated products, all of them delivered down the one wire.

Many analysts feel, however, that if the old British Telecom could have avoided the split and instead could have forged a number of significant partnerships with firms abroad, it might have been at the centre of a far greater keiretsu than it is today.

What it takes for a company to succeed

There are two types of successful company today. One is the keiretsu with a strong brand and a pro-active attitude to anticipating consumers' needs. The other is the supplier/designer that is perpetually nimble and manages to remain world class. To some extent it is up to the keiretsu to see that its own network of suppliers (which it manages) stays world class and is not allowed to become complacent.

Another crucial element for a successful keiretsu is to have a thorough understanding of its customers. Most analysts agree that success today stands or falls on a firm's relationship with its customers. Keiretsus must know how to anticipate their customers' needs, and they must have the ability to respond rapidly to those needs.

That puts a heavy burden on electronic communication: that between the keiretsu to which the company belongs and its customers; and that between members of the same keiretsu. Business is won by groups that can bring together the diffuse bits of their organisation in a way and at a speed that enables them to create better and faster solutions to consumers' needs than anyone else. This puts a premium on speedy efficient intranets. Many of today's most successful groups made heavy investments in their network infrastructure in the 1990s.

The complexity of these networks is extraordinary, and successful groups have to be extremely skilled at managing them. Some of the most highly paid executives in business today work in the central office of a keiretsu, the place where the alliances between the individual members of the group are nurtured, and where strategic decisions about the development of the networks are taken. (Incidentally, the word 'headquarters' is no longer considered appropriate as a name for the place where these central functions are carried out.)

Early warning signs

There were a number of early warning signals at the beginning of this century to suggest that the Keiretsu Rising scenario was the one most likely to unfold over the following decade. For example, it was easy to see at the end of the 1990s that a great many of the alliances that were being formed between companies were designed expressly to increase the range of products that each was able to offer.

A great many financial institutions, for example, linked up with supermarkets both in Europe and North America. This enabled the supermarkets to offer loans that helped customers to buy more of their goods. And it enabled the banks to sell their customers a few cosmetics while they waited to have a talk with the manager.

Then airlines linked up with the banks and the supermarkets, and they began to sell the products of the other two via their in-flight entertainment systems. Bored passengers with nothing better to do on long journeys were able to shop at an electronic mall while flying at 33,000 feet above sea level.

Another clear signal was given by the way in which companies from different industries started to come together in order to consolidate their market positions. There were a number of particularly significant deals—such as that in 2001 between the Prudential insurance company of America and Bloomingdales, the upmarket New York department store. The Prudential handed over to Bloomingdales the task of replacing all the goods that customers claimed under its household insurance policies.

This gave the Prudential an edge in selling policies because its customers were told that whatever they lost would be replaced with Bloomingdales' top-class products. At the same time it gave Bloomingdales a boost by making it the sole supplier of replacement goods to Prudential policyholders. In the first full year that the deal was in operation, Bloomingdales' turnover increased by almost 50%.

At about the same time there were a number of cases where groups of disparate companies launched joint loyalty programmes. One of the most widely publicised was that between British Petroleum, the Body Shop and the Virgin group. Customers of any of these organisations gained points in the scheme and could set them off against the price of goods from any of the other suppliers. They could also, alternatively, get lottery tickets. One customer who bought a Body Shop footbath in 1999 also won £12 million on Britain's national lottery.

Another sign of the rise of the keiretsu came from the way in which new entrants into markets were increasingly able to compete only in very small niches. Whereas at one time all sorts of traditional industries—from banking to computer manufacturing—were inundated with newcomers who seemed able to grab significant market share in next to no time, that phenomenon gradually disappeared. Markets came to be dominated by a few keiretsu and by the organisations that were part of them. Whereas in the late 1990s, for example, 80% of the European car-seat market was accounted for by 12 different manufacturers, by 2003 90% of that market was supplied by a mere five manufacturers.

Eventually the only way that newcomers could survive outside the big conglomerates was by finding a very small niche where there was a narrowly defined need that the conglomerates had chosen not to satisfy. There is one small independent firm, for example, that produces a software program to do a spell check in Latvian. It has not yet found that it needs to be part of a larger group.

Likewise, some health-food products which make use of rare plants found only in remote parts of China are not generally supplied by any of the big conglomerates. They are happy to leave the business to a couple of small specialist firms based in Hong Kong that know it intimately. By and large, however, firms have found that they freeze to death if they stay too long outside the shelter of one of the big keiretsu.

Chapter summary

In this chapter I have described a scenario in which the industrial world is dominated by a fairly small number of giant keiretsu, networks of highly specialised organisations which come together to meet the needs of extremely demanding customers. These customers want products that are tailored for them. They don't want the output of mass markets, they want products made for a market of one.

Customers work with the keiretsus to design and produce jointly the exact products that meet their individual needs. The keiretsus manage a network of suppliers who between them aim to supply customers with the products and services that they demand. The keiretsu is the interface between suppliers and customers. So it is in the keiretsu's interest to see that all the suppliers within its network maintain world-class standards and do not become complacent.

From within its own network, a single keiretsu will be able to satisfy a very wide range of goods and services. The Barclays Group, for instance, supplies everything from loans to fresh flowers. Customer loyalty is one key to success, and keiretsus compete fiercely in order to lock customers into their particular distribution channel and into the products and services to which it gives access.

Branding is essential, and all the big keiretsu operate behind a major brand—Ford, Barclays, Shell, etc. This helps to give customers confidence in the whole range of products within the group.

Another critical factor in enabling firms to meet the demands of customers is information technology. Successful keiretsu have sophisticated interactive electronic channels which go right into consumers' homes. And they have intranets which enable the member firms of each keiretsu to communicate among themselves. High-speed and high-content communication is at the heart of all successful business today.

6

Acme & Co

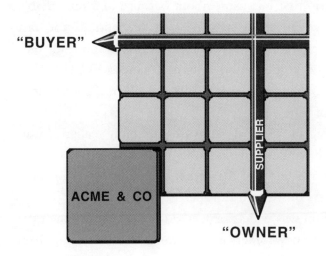

"BUYER"

SUPPLIER

ACME & CO

"OWNER"

OUR THIRD SCENARIO LIES IN THE BOTTOM LEFT-HAND corner of the window made by our two axes. In this scenario suppliers extend their reach further and further along the value chain, and consumers indicate very clearly that they prefer to choose from a multitude of pre-prepared products, and then to base their choice overwhelmingly on price.

Companies rarely attempt to be very narrow specialists, focused on only one link in the value chain; and consumers show little inclination to become involved in the creation of personalised products to meet their needs.

We have called this scenario Acme & Co, and it is characterised by extremely large, vertically integrated companies that compete fiercely for market share. In effect, everything is much as it was ten years ago, only bigger.

It is a scenario that has come about because of a remarkable reversal of fortune. In most industries at the end of the last century, nimble newcomers were running rings around old-established firms. A combination of circumstances enabled them to capture significant market share from established players in a very short space of time.

For instance, in 1999 a software company called Intuit entered the retail banking market and in less than 18 months managed to grab over 20% of the personal loan business in some of the main markets of western Europe.

This revolution was widely expected to continue in much the same direction, with newcomers over-running traditional suppliers across the board. But then, in an extraordinary volte-face, the likes of which have never been seen before or since, the revolution suddenly changed direction around the beginning of this century.

The old-established industry leaders finally decided to do something about the intruders. Still strong, rich and determined, they decided to cancel the party before it got out of hand. The beginnings of this movement could be seen as long ago as 1998 when, within the space of a few weeks, a number of the biggest banks in America merged with each other. The biggest deal was between Citicorp and Travelers Group. But, in all, over $400 billion-worth of deals were put together in under a month.

In 2000 the trend became even more pronounced. A sizeable group of companies—all of them in *Fortune*'s list of the world's

500 biggest corporations—then made a number of large-scale leveraged buy-outs. In many cases these involved companies from the Fortune 500 ranking buying other companies high up the *Fortune* list.

Initially this was a defensive response by organisations looking to protect their existing market shares. These organisations still had access to vast pools of capital, and they used that access in order to buy other big companies that they hoped would reinforce their market positions.

As a strategy, it succeeded far beyond the companies' wildest dreams. With each other's help, they soon found themselves able to claw back market share—largely by paring their prices to the bone and discovering that consumers cared for little else.

For that was the key to their success. Consumers had become extremely price conscious, and the new entrants' ability to undercut the prices of the old timers had been the main driver behind their early triumph. The newcomers could keep their prices down because they were free of some of the heavy costs that their predecessors had to bear. They did not need to build the same infrastructure, for example, and this had made them powerful competitors in a number of utilities

Then again, in many of the service industries that had traditionally been run from a chain of expensive offices or branches, the newcomers found that they could do without such overheads, selling their services by phone or by mail. And finally, deregulation freed them from many of the constraints that had applied to the old-timers. For example, the need to provide universal coverage—a telephone line to every village, or piped water to every household—did not apply to them.

When the old-timers fully realised what was happening, they found that they had a powerful weapon with which to fight back. Their ever-increasing size enabled them to reap more and more economies of scale, and the new mega-corporations were thus able to compete fairly and squarely on the same playing field as the newcomers, a playing field called 'price'.

The pressure quickly proved too much for most of the newcomers to handle. They soon discovered that there was always a conglomerate prepared to undercut them for just as long as it took to put them out of business.

By 2002, a combination of the mergers and take-overs of the Fortune 500 companies, and intensive government lobbying by the traditional industry players, had beaten back most of the newcomers. Concerned about the possibility of repeat attacks, however, the old firms continued to buy other companies, intending to build buffer zones around themselves. Mostly they bought companies from within their own industry, but they also occasionally bought companies from other industries.

A large number of household names disappeared during this period. In 2006, for example, of the 500 companies in the Fortune 500 list, only just over half had been on the same list two years previously. There was no precedent for this sort of turnover in the whole of industrial history.

The effect of the fight back by the old timers on the average size of companies was amazing. A few hundred companies around the world became vast giants. And they created an enormous chasm between themselves and the next biggest companies. Not only were impudent newcomers crushed by the awesome market power of the new conglomerates, but fewer and fewer companies of medium size found it possible to exist outside the shelter of the giants.

This had an adverse effect on the many companies from developing countries that were just beginning at the end of the last century to make inroads into western markets. For they were treated by the behemoths in the same way as if they had been impudent newcomers from the industrialised world. The successful ones were gobbled up and integrated into the conglomerates; the less successful ones were forced out of business.

At one time it had seemed as if the developing world was about to bring its new companies and products to the developed world. But the corporate behemoths reversed all that and carried the battle to the developing countries. They then set out to influence legislation in those countries in a direction that continued to let the local markets mature, but not at the expense of the behemoths themselves.

In that, they have been reasonably successful. Although each giant conglomerate has a strong regional affinity of its own, most of them have their particular strength in North America, Europe or East Asia. Royal Dutch Shell is European, for example; Ford is American; and Mitsubishi is East Asian. There are very few conglomerates with their main regional strength in Africa or the Middle East. These regions are served by conglomerates that are based elsewhere.

There have been occasional cries of protest at what some have described as the 'neo-colonialism' of the conglomerates. Barclays' services were boycotted around the world after widespread screening of a popular television drama set in the South Africa of the 1960s and 1970s. It showed how Barclays had continued to operate in the country during the time of apartheid.

But the Barclays boycott did not last long. The protesters soon realised that they were having little effect on governments because most consumers (i.e., most voters) were more concerned with price than with history. And in several important market segments Barclays' prices were (and still are) unbeatable. Consumers took the opportunity to demonstrate unequivocally that they were not prepared to allow politics to get in the way of a good bargain.

Despite the proven resilience of the large conglomerates, none of them are yet prepared to rest on their laurels. Their experience in the last few years of the last century was too traumatic to be forgotten quickly, and even today they continue to merge and acquire each other in a never-ending effort to fortify their positions even further.

A few of these leading corporations cut across traditional industry boundaries. During a seven-month spell in 2001, for example, Royal Dutch Shell acquired Federal Express, an international courier business, Mercury, the UK's second biggest telecoms company, and Tesco, then Britain's favourite supermarket. And the giant conglomerate has continued to make major purchases ever since in order to reap yet more economies of scale. It is currently negotiating to acquire three offshore exploration firms.

Shell's annual revenues are now well in excess of $250 billion, and its annual spending on consulting alone is enough to keep many firms afloat. But Shell is no longer an oil company. Indeed, oil and petrochemicals now account for less than a quarter of the Anglo–Dutch giant's total sales.

Few conglomerates have branched out as widely as Shell. Indeed, most have not diversified beyond a quite narrow range of products and services. But this has been enough to undermine many traditional systems of industrial classification. In Shell's case, for example, it is hard to know whether to classify it as an oil, a petrochemicals, a retailing, a telecoms or a transport company.

The consumer's point of view

The overriding feature of consumers in the year 2008 is their price consciousness. But this has not come about because consumers are in general poorer than they used to be. Steady growth across the industrial world, and less steady growth in the developing world, have helped to raise standards of living all over. They have not, however, risen to such an extent (or with such suddenness) that people have felt tempted to go on the sort of spending binges that are now historically associated with the 1980s.

Commentators keep saying that people 'feel poorer' than they used to, even though statistics show quite clearly that they aren't. This feeling of (relative) poverty is evidenced by things like the sharp fall in the sale of luxury goods over the past few years—of fine wines and Swiss watches in particular.

Some have suggested that this is because the role of the state in the life of the individual has been rolled back in recent years. People have to pay for many things nowadays that used to be provided free—for a start, the education of their children, their own retirement and old age, and their own health care. Today these things have to be paid for out of voluntary savings rather than out of compulsory taxes. And consumers seem to feel poorer when making these necessary savings than they did when paying the required taxes.

In many ways the success of the large megastores of the 1990s set the trend for contemporary consumer values. In the last decade of the last century customers wheeled their wire baskets up and down enormously long corridors beside which were arrayed the products of hundreds of manufacturers. The key things that consumers looked for then were price and convenience—they wanted to meet as many of their regular shopping needs in one store as possible. And they wanted no frills. Frills meant higher prices . . . and customers knew it.

Today the no-frills philosophy has been taken to extremes. Packaging, for example, is very simple, and only essential information about a product is displayed. There is little hype or glamour. The relationship between customer and supplier is focused solely on the product purchased.

Consumers, however, no longer traipse up and down the corridors of megastores. A typical worker today does most of his or her shopping electronically. They settle their bills at the end of each month by sending electronic payments for things like their car and their food to a company like Barclays. Their electricity, gas, water and phone bills are likely to be all settled with a single company such as British Utilities.

After a worker's accounts have been paid by Microsoft eCheque, he or she might typically spot an on-line advertisement from Toyota offering new attractive discounts on international calls to Japan. Workers who have reason to make frequent calls to Japan only need to send an electronic message informing British Utilities that they are cancelling their phone service. They then send another message to ask Toyota Voice to connect them. The whole process of switching telephone suppliers these days does not need to take more than a few minutes.

Another big change for the consumer from 15 years ago is the little differentiation that there is between products. Cars, for example, all tend to look the same, and the rates and conditions of financial services are scarcely distinguishable from one vendor to another. This has come about partly because all companies rapidly adopt any new technique for cutting costs, and over the years this has tended to make their output more and more similar. Fierce competition has also discouraged firms from going out of line with the rest of the pack.

Since there is now little difference between the products of one organisation and those of another, customers naturally tend to be guided by the brand names that they trust. And trust resides most strongly these days with regional firms. A European customer trying to choose between Unilever No 5 washing powder, say, and P&G's Press and Go powder is almost certain to choose the Unilever brand. Needless to say, the price and chemical constitution of both products is virtually identical.

In general, though, the price consciousness of consumers does not allow them to show much 'loyalty' to any one brand when its prices fall out of line. They are more than happy to switch suppliers whenever price variations make it worth their while. Flashy promotions occur frequently and offer short-term price discounts. But they tend to have only a temporary effect on sales, and they rarely persuade consumers to switch products over the longer term.

The view from the marketplace

The technological revolution, which promised so much in the 1990s, never fulfilled its promise. For sure, the major conglomerates are able to reach customers everywhere thanks to their sophisticated knowledge management systems. And high-tech gizmos have certainly made the front end of business, where firms interact with their customers, much prettier. Mail-order catalogues downloaded via the Internet now show products in remarkably life-like three-dimensional virtual reality. This allows customers to do everything but feel the goods that they are being enticed to buy.

The real battles, however, take place behind these prettily designed multimedia facades. Any big money being spent on information technology today is going into supporting manufacturing processes, into transactions handling, and into upgrading back-office systems. There is a strong emphasis also on internal, private networking.

The ability to move information throughout an organisation quickly and efficiently is often the main thing that differentiates one company from another. So private networks have become a key way for companies to gain competitive advantage.

The multinational conglomerate Sears, Roebuck, for instance, has made a name for itself by designing a proprietary network that is widely recognised as the most efficient in the business. Other firms have taken tremendous pains to copy it, and

Sears only manages to stay one step ahead by continually coming up with new improvements.

At Sears, as at other companies, research and development expenditure is concentrated on finding new systems and new production processes that allow the company to trim its prices, however marginally. Little R&D effort goes into developing new products or services. So there is only a trickle of new products appearing on the market.

When an innovative idea does appear it is quickly imitated, and any cost advantage that the innovator might have gained rapidly disappears. The cycle of cost reduction and price wars then starts all over again.

Regulation

In the world of Acme & Co there is a big role for regulators. Strong nationalistic and protectionist sentiments in many of the world's major markets have resulted in a slowdown in the sort of global openness that was heralded by liberal organisations such as NAFTA, the North American Free Trade Area, and WTO, the World Trade Organisation. The European Union has done nothing to counter this trend.

The current EU government is intensely conservative, and it sometimes seems set on keeping things as close as possible to the way they were in the 1990s. The EU's reaction to most evidence of rapid change is one of 'wait and see' ... and so far there has been a lot more waiting than seeing. The EU's proposals for a social contract between employers and employees, for example, are still collecting dust more than a quarter of a century after they were first proposed.

The EU has undoubtedly been a powerful influence in creating the regional blocs that now dominate the business world. It has changed markedly from the outward looking organisation of the 1990s that wanted to increase its membership and expand its sphere of influence almost without limit within the Christian world. Now it is an introverted organisation that is primarily concerned with the narrow self-interest of its own members and with maintaining the status quo.

Regulation in the EU, as elsewhere, is overwhelmingly in favour of large monolithic organisations and existing market structures. Nimble newcomers almost invariably get bogged down in rules that are largely designed to protect the interests of a particular geographic region. Not for 30 years have people in business talked so much about 'red tape'.

Industry incumbents have lobbied hard (and often successfully) for the retention of policies in their favour. All the big conglomerates have large budgets for lobbying policy-makers around the world, and this has inevitably led to widespread accusations of bribery. Newspapers seem to be even more full of stories about graft and corruption than they were in the 1990s.

Some people have pointed out that this policy of favouring big business has not only throttled new enterprise and new ideas, but that it has also worked to the detriment of wider environmental and social programmes. In the EU there has been little progress made on either of these in recent years.

Big business has fought hard against anything that might increase the cost of labour. So, for example, new legislation on a minimum wage has inevitably been stalled wherever attempts have been made to introduce it. Trade union rights have been nibbled away; and things such as statutory paternity leave and worker representation on company boards have been put on a back burner—and have never come to the boil.

There have been occasional demonstrations of protest against this lack of development. But the power of the conglomerates is so great that employees fear that they may lose their ability to earn a living if they demonstrate against something that is part of corporate policy. In a notorious case in the United States, two employees of a very large conglomerate were sacked for attempting to organise a union at their place of work. They claimed in court that they were subsequently blackballed by a large number of alternative potential employers who had been influenced in their action by the firm that had originally sacked them.

Despite strong evidence in their favour—including taped conversations between the chairmen of two of the conglomerates about the need to do 'whatever is necessary' to keep wage costs down—the two lost their case. It did, however, go all the way to the Supreme Court.

As with social policy, so with the environment. The conglomerates are constantly being tempted to cut corners in their remorseless efforts to save costs. No one today sees any merit in the argument that being environmentally responsible is good for business. Consumers literally won't buy it. Although they do claim in surveys to be concerned about the environment, they are rarely prepared to pay even a penny extra for a product that claims to be environmentally friendly.

Pioneers in the area, like The Body Shop, have gone out of business. The last of The Body Shop's retail outlets (located in a small town in central Wales) was closed three years ago. Today the site has become something of a shrine for the few who still dare to express concern about the way in which the world is being polluted by industrial production.

Many of the most telling indicators of pollution have been rising in recent years, after having fallen consistently for a decade before that. Pollutants in some of the major rivers in Europe, for instance, have risen so high that many traditional fishing grounds are now completely lifeless.

More and more, however, governments turn a blind eye on the environmental damage caused by the conglomerates.

Everybody is well aware of the fundamental clash between the desire to protect the environment and the desire to further economic growth. The EU's recent dismantling of its environmental ministry has served only to highlight this dilemma—and the way in which it is, in general, being resolved.

Industry's point of view

The most obvious trend within industry over the past ten years has been the growing concentration of production in the hands of a few corporate behemoths. This has been achieved by means of a remarkable increase in the number of mergers and acquisitions both inside and outside traditional industry boundaries.

For several years at the beginning of this decade, mergers and acquisitions around the world more than doubled each year in both number and value. And it did not take long for this to have a marked effect on the structure of industry. For example, the gross revenues of *Fortune* magazine's top 100 companies more than doubled in ten years.

The big got very much bigger; but the small didn't. And to such an extent that the regeneration rate of companies today is negative—i.e. more companies are being closed down than are being started up.

New entrants into businesses are almost invariably large companies. The significant barriers standing in the way of new entrants—in the shape of red tape and of the considerable investment required to make a start—effectively eliminate the small entrepreneur from having a go at most things. The large entrenched conglomerates own the entirety of many different value-chains, from raw materials to distribution and selling.

And they are in no mood to yield any ground whatsoever. They have frequently shown themselves to be ruthless in the way that they cut prices to eliminate newcomers. On many occasions they have spent heavily on advertising their price cuts just at a time when a potentially competitive product was being launched.

Almost all legislation designed to prevent price discrimination between one consumer and another has been repealed. Conglomerates are always seeking to take advantage of shifts in markets to improve their margins. When, for example, the last tweed mill in Ireland closed down recently, the two other significant suppliers in the country immediately increased their prices by exactly 40%. Nobody bothered to question such a coincidence.

The two firms' prices in England, however, remained unchanged because they continued to have real competition there. But in the time that it took for arbitrageurs to ship tweed from England to Ireland in order to take advantage of the price difference, the two original suppliers had made a handsome profit. They then pared their prices right back when the arbitrageurs began to make serious inroads into their market.

Geographical regions are typically dominated in this way by oligopolies of local suppliers. In many regions of the developing world these oligopolies consist of suppliers that are in fact owned by conglomerates in the developed world. But they frequently go to great lengths to disguise the fact.

Exploitation of emerging economies is critical in the price-focused markets in which conglomerates operate today. In the West they face stagnant growth; so it is only in the developing world that they can hope to sustain reasonable margins for any length of time.

Consequently, most companies in the West send their most able people—and their investment dollars—to places such as India, China and the countries of the former Soviet Union. There they hope to be able to find new ways to generate revenue streams in relatively untapped markets.

MBA courses at business schools in the West almost always include a compulsory language module, and the most popular languages on these courses for some years now have been Cantonese and Russian. In universities there has been a remarkable growth in the number of undergraduate courses that combine business studies and the Turkish language. Graduates of these courses have little problem finding jobs with western companies in fast-expanding central Asian republics such as Kazakhstan, Azerbaijan and Turkmenistan.

What famous companies are doing

Many familiar companies from the 1990s now look very different. The Nokia Telecom Company, for example, has successfully expanded into a number of different non-traditional markets around the globe. Its period of expansion started in 1998 after it had released its proprietary Nokiachip 980, a microchip embedded in its telecom products that enabled minor technical corrections to be made to the product itself by means of electronic codes transmitted through traditional telephone lines.

Anxious to improve on the success of this chip and its cellular phone business, Nokia began acquiring local telecoms providers in the early months of 2002. Today, in addition to being a big player in consumer electronics, the company runs the fifth largest telecoms business in the world.

Likewise the Ford Motor Company has expanded into a large number of non-traditional markets around the world. In the late 1990s the company leveraged its immense size and capital reserves to expand rapidly. Deciding that it really could be 'all things to all people', Ford began its expansion with a foray into retail financial services. Its Ford Credit Operation was immensely successful and was the harbinger of a monolithic company that now offers its customers everything from cars to telephony.

One of the company's most successful ventures has been its

theme parks. Modelled on the Disney leisure villages, there are now a dozen such parks around the world. The latest one was opened earlier this year just outside Moscow.

Called Ford Car Parks, they are based on the history of the car and all its aspects. Visitors stay in hotels on the site and are able to enjoy a drive in a Grand Prix car. They are also offered simulated drives in cars of the past and of the future.

Special exhibits include famous drives from films and literature. One of the most popular is a virtual reality drive from downtown Manhattan to the home of Gatsby as described in F. Scott FitzGerald's ever popular *The Great Gatsby*. Another popular ride is a simulated ticker-tape welcome down New York's Fifth Avenue.

Ford was able to expand its range of businesses very easily because of the lessons it learnt early on about how to keep costs under control in a global operation. Many companies found that they could be highly competitive in Western Europe and North America, where long experience had taught them how to run a tight ship. But once they spread into the new markets of Asia and Latin America, many of them lost their competitive edge. Some of them even lost their shirt. To keep costs down in these markets, they found, required a deep understanding of their cultures.

Barclays is another company that has managed to make a successful transition from being a single industry firm in the twentieth century to becoming a jack-of-several-trades in the twenty-first. It is sometimes hard to remember that in the early 1990s Barclays was exclusively a bank. Today it is a sort of financial megastore selling every kind of financial service.

The company skilfully anticipated the profound changes that took place at the turn of the century in the banking industry— changes that wiped out many of its long-time rivals. And it was able to control its costs rather better than its rivals by the simple expedient of closing down all its high-street branches. These had traditionally been located at some of the most expensive points on the UK's major shopping streets.

In their place, Barclays opened a number of strategically located call centres which its customers could contact by phone, free of charge. These centres were originally situated in areas of the UK where there was a plentiful supply of cheap labour. But Barclays quickly realised that its customer base was expanding well beyond the UK. Customers from all over the world soon began to appreciate the low cost and high quality of its services, and it was not difficult for them to tap into the Barclays network.

Thereafter a growing number of Barclays call centres (and its Internet service centres) moved to even cheaper locations in other parts of the world. The company now provides English-language telephone services throughout the world, 24 hours a day, from major hubs in Zimbabwe, the Falkland Islands and Cairns in northern Australia.

In addition, the company has opened a number of offices in the centres of major cities. These are usually situated on the first or second floor of inexpensive buildings. But they are carefully chosen for their proximity to major transport hubs.

This has a dual purpose. First of all it makes it convenient for customers to pop in whenever they have to wait at, say, an airport or a railway terminal. And secondly, it allows Barclays to display its blue and white logo prominently in a position where it can be seen by the many thousands of travellers who pass through these hubs.

Many of the traditional utilities have also gone through a major transformation in recent years. Deregulation in the 1990s introduced some fundamental changes to their industries, and they presented firms with some remarkable new opportunities.

British Gas, the UK's monopoly gas provider, was one company that took some of these opportunities. Towards the end of 1999 it began a pilot scheme in the south-west of London that provided homes in the area with electricity and telephone services.

British Gas purchased these services in bulk from long-established providers.

The company promised that its prices would always be below those of the traditional suppliers, and it adopted a slogan that had been made popular by the John Lewis Partnership: 'Never knowingly undersold'.

The scheme was an instant success. So many customers signed up for the low-cost services that the company soon changed its name to British Utilities. It added new services to its range—water, for instance, and waste disposal—and in 2004 began to offer the whole range right across the United Kingdom.

Apart from its extremely competitive pricing, British Utilities (BU) has gained a competitive edge by coming out with a highly innovative range of appliances. Not only do these use BU products, but they also have the ability to communicate with the company through its gas, telephone and power lines.

This communication allows BU to monitor the consumption of the appliance (for billing purposes and for market research). And it also allows BU to spot problems that arise with the appliances or with the supply of BU products. In certain cases the company can send electronic instructions via these communications links, and the instructions are themselves enough to fix the problem.

This has led to a remarkable fall in the number of service people employed by BU. Nowadays its customers rarely need a home visit from a service agent, the sort of person whose little white vans were a familiar sight clogging up the streets of major cities ten years ago.

There is at least one large company that we can find, however, that has not changed much over the past ten years. British Telecom has remained at heart a telecoms business despite all the new opportunities that came with its privatisation and the subsequent deregulation of the industry.

The company has remained profitable and has managed to hang on to its customers by matching its rivals on price. Compensating for its lower margins has been a vast increase in volumes—it is estimated that usage of telephone lines in the UK (both speech and modem) has increased four-fold over the past ten years.

However, in other parts of the world the growth in volumes has been far in excess of this. Countries like Thailand and South Africa, for instance, have seen usage increase several hundred-fold. In general, BT has failed to grasp new opportunities outside its domestic market.

The company has realised, however, that it cannot stand still. Telecoms is a very competitive business, and most of the big conglomerates have some sort of presence in it. Those that don't, almost to a man, have plans to enter the industry soon.

So BT is actively pursuing other lines of business in a search for better margins. It has a small multimedia production company and it is continually broadening the range of the off-the-shelf telecoms products that it manufactures. These include pagers, printers, video-conferencing machines, and a number of increasingly sophisticated telephones.

What it takes for a company to be successful

Winning companies today are masters of re-engineering and cost reduction. The management fashion for re-engineering, which began in the recession of the early 1990s, died down in the later years of that decade. But it has been revived in the twenty-first century with a vengeance.

Successful companies have to be of such size and scope that they can choose to squash almost any newcomer that attempts to enter their markets. To remain in that position they have to be involved in a process of continual re-engineering that tirelessly seeks out new ways for them to cut costs. They also have to look continually for new and better ways to learn from their experience, to apply to one market what they have found out in another. The successful dinosaurs have proved time and again that experience and size can overcome nimbleness and speed in getting a product to market.

The dinosaurs also gain competitive advantage from the sophisticated information systems that they have developed to keep them up to date on their customers' needs. All big firms take pride in their knowledge of the very latest demographic trends, and most advertise that knowledge in their marketing campaigns.

The importance of information systems to firms has persuaded them to try and whip up a degree of loyalty in those employees who know how to design and run these systems. This they do by entering into 'social contracts' with key employees. These make certain guarantees about levels of employment and, in an increasing number of cases, about the conglomerate's environmental responsibility too.

Andersen Consulting has remained successful in this scenario by becoming a large behemoth organisation itself. Nowadays it counts most of the big industry incumbents as its clients, and it has a world-wide staff of more than 100,000 people. The firm is heavily involved in helping organisations to integrate their mergers and acquisitions by providing them with strategy advice and with other business information services.

Andersen Consulting's investment banking practice has also proved to be extremely successful. The firm has identified and recommended many acquisition targets for its clients, and it has also helped to fund much of their M&A activity. Andersen Consulting regularly appears in lists of the top ten 'investment banks' in Europe and the United States.

The early warning signs

With the benefit of hindsight it is clear that there were a number of signs at the beginning of this century to indicate that the future of industry was going to lie in the hands of a small number of vast conglomerates doing everything from A to Z.

In the first instance there was an ever-increasing number of acquisitions, both within industries and across industries. In the late 1990s both the number and the value of these acquisitions increased dramatically. The biggest deal by value in the 1980s was worth around $25 billion; the biggest deal in the 1990s was worth over $150 billion; while the biggest deal so far this decade was worth (in 1999 dollars) just under $500 billion. In addition, so far this decade there have been another 50 deals worth $300 billion or more.

These deals have occurred not only between giant firms in the same industry—in chemicals, banking and computers, for instance—but also between giant firms in different (though usually related) industries. The two biggest Swiss banks joined together in 1997, and then they acquired the biggest Swiss insurance company. Finally, the resulting conglomerate merged with Switzerland's biggest supermarket chain.

All these mergers and acquisitions quickly concentrated industrial sales in the hands of a few very large firms. In many major economies today the markets for quite significant consumer products are effectively supplied by just two or three producers.

Some indication of this growing concentration can be gleaned from the fact that the aggregate revenue of the top 100 companies in the world doubled in real terms between 1997 and 2007. A chart of that growth shows that it took place quite evenly over the period, except that there was a quantum leap between 1998 and 1999. In that year the mergers between the giant firms first made their impact felt.

Finally, the shape of things to come could have been detected from the way in which new entrants into industries seemed increasingly to be large companies, not small ones. In the 1990s many industry pundits had predicted that information technology was going to make it possible for very small new businesses to take on established giants in a wide range of industries. And, as we have seen, for a while that did occur. The most famous example, perhaps, was Netscape, an American company that invented a browser for searching the World Wide Web and that momentarily had over 60% of a world market worth several billions. But Netscape was soon crushed by the large industrial conglomerates that were attracted to its business . . . and its (briefly) handsome margins.

In practice, small firms have had to struggle for all of this century. It is the big conglomerates that have gone into new markets and new businesses, and that have taken on the established firms in those businesses. Ford Worldwide challenges Walt Disney in one of its core businesses, and British Utilities takes on British Telecom in a market that, within living memory, BT had almost entirely to itself.

Chapter summary

In this chapter I have described a scenario that we call Acme & Co. In it, the dominant features are the price consciousness of consumers and the size of the vast conglomerates that dominate the industrial landscape.

In the late 1990s it appeared that the combination of deregulation, rapid advances in technology, and shifting demographics was going to create an environment in which small new firms could enter markets dominated by big old-established businesses, and could then snatch significant market share from under their noses in less time than it took to write a new strategic plan.

But that proved to be a false dawn. Before long the old-established industries had fought back. In a tidal wave of breathtaking mergers and acquisitions, a hundred or so of the world's biggest companies suddenly got very much bigger, and they opened up a wide gap between themselves and what could be described as medium-sized firms.

Today the industrial world is dominated by these giants, and they control a number of different value chains in their entirety. Although they are global in their reach, each of them has a strong regional home base which they defend fiercely by intensively lobbying local governments. It is not widely realised, however, that in the developing world many of the regional giants are in practice owned by western conglomerates.

Governments everywhere are in favour of big business, and most of them turn a blind eye to breaches of anti-trust regulations. Nevertheless, there is a large volume of regulation that is largely designed to protect local markets. Indeed, small firms say that there has never been so much red tape within living memory.

However, the regulation carefully avoids areas that might add to Big Business's costs—employment legislation, for example, or environmental controls.

The chapter looks at a number of conglomerates that were household names ten years ago and describes what has happened to them in the meanwhile. The Ford Motor Company has changed its name to Ford Worldwide; Barclays Bank has dropped the 'Bank'. All of those that have thrived are now offering a far wider range of goods and services than they were in the 1990s.

Consumers are fickle in their search for the best price, and they 'shop around' shamelessly. So firms are compelled to shave costs wherever possible. The companies that succeed in this scenario are masters of re-engineering and cost cutting.

In every industry today, imitators follow the leaders so quickly that any cost advantage is almost always clawed back in a very short space of time, and there is a never-ending cycle of cost cutting and copying.

Firms offer customers a range of no frills predefined products from which to choose. But there is little to differentiate one conglomerate's product range from another.

Companies' research and development expenditure is focused on finding new processes and systems that can be used to cut costs. Innovative new products and services are rare, partly because they can be imitated so quickly that investment in innovation is scarcely ever able to reap a reasonable return.

Finally, the chapter looks at whether there were any early warning signals that could have been spotted a few years ago, and that would have indicated the evolution of an Acme & Co scenario.

It suggests that there were three:

✦ First, there was the very obvious growth in M&A activity both within and across industries.

✦ Secondly, there was the fact that the gross revenues of the world's 100 biggest companies (taken from *Fortune* magazine's listing) doubled in real terms within ten years. That was a sure indication that the structure of industry was undergoing a major upheaval.

✦ Finally, there was the fact that new entrants into various growth industries seemed more and more to be large companies. Small and entrepreneurial businesses were very evidently getting squashed by the increasing power of the conglomerates.

7

Excelliance

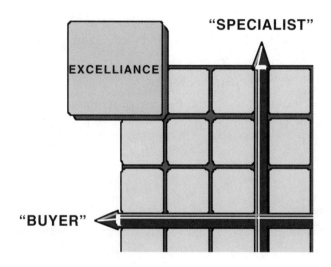

T HE FOURTH SCENARIO WE HAVE CALLED EXCELLIANCE, A
combination of the words 'excellent' and 'alliance'. It is a
world where companies have to be supreme experts at whatever
they choose to do, and where they have to form a multitude of
alliances with other experts at different points in the value chain in
order to produce goods and services for the marketplace.

In this world there is fierce competition between

organisations. Margins are continually being squeezed and stock markets are more demanding than ever. Any way to get ahead and gain an advantage over competitors is eagerly seized upon, and the amount of scandal in business has never been higher. All over the world business ethics appear to be at an all-time low.

The intense competition extends across the whole of the value chain. Nike, Virgin and other marketing firms are perpetually rolling out new promotions and incentives in their attempts to entice people into their stores and onto their on-line malls. It is a world in which consumers have too many choices (from veteran players and newcomers alike) for companies to be able to rely on old-fashioned customer loyalty.

Global legislation and a global system of regulation have combined with open technical standards, and these have helped suppliers to form alliances with others who are able to take care of functions that lie outside their own core competence. The perpetual need to produce products of a consistently high quality ensures that these alliances are formal and long term.

Old industry categories no longer exist. Firms that focus on excellence in a narrow range of skills work right across the spectrum of industry and commerce. Organisations now concentrate on a core competence, and there are new roles for so-called 'value chain integrators', firms that package individual components in the value chain.

Technology has been a key element in shaping this new business model. For organisations hoping to bring a product to market, it is essential to develop communications links with partner companies. And these links need to be upgraded as the relationship changes throughout the life cycle of the product. So-called 'collaboration support tools', which provide on-the-spot links between different players in the value chain, have become a key market for business integrators.

The new global playing field has also finally brought an end to government subsidies. World markets are now characterised by prices that truly reflect costs. But industries are growing weary under the strain. Last year the EU tried to impose a new set of tariffs on goods and services coming from outside its borders. Consumer protests eventually stopped the move, but some analysts believe that the EU and others will soon take steps to renationalise markets in order to regain control of some parts of the value chain.

Consumers

Over the past few years consumers have become extremely demanding. They want excellence, and they want it now. They want to buy things 'off the shelf' and are not prepared to wait for them to be customised. (Although the expression 'off the shelf' remains in common usage, there are in fact few shelves left in this the age of eCommerce.)

Consumers want high quality and service, and they want it at a low price. There is an old saw that is very apt today: 'It's not cheaper things that we want to possess, but expensive things that cost a lot less.' Consumers are very price conscious, avidly searching on-line shopping malls for the cheapest version of whatever it is that they want.

The steadily increasing demands of consumers have had some undesirable side effects. Litigation against manufacturers who produce products that are unsafe, or which fall seriously short of what they claim to be, began with the consumer movement in the United States. It forced some firms to pay compensation for outrageous cases of negligence, and it kept all manufacturers on their toes.

But consumer litigation has now reached a stage where it is frequently working against consumers' interests. For example, for some years it has been almost impossible to find a children's playground in a public place in America. So severe were the compensation payments demanded by the courts in a number of cases where children were hurt while on playground equipment, that no local authority or park management company is prepared any longer to take the risk.

The only way that consumers can buy such equipment now is in kit form. This they have to assemble themselves for use in the privacy of their own homes or gardens.

Even then they have to be careful whom they invite to use the equipment. Some parents demand that friends and neighbours sign an agreement before they allow their children to come and play. The agreement says that the parents give up their right to seek compensation if their children are harmed.

A similar development has taken place in the market for light aircraft. Such planes are now almost invariably bought in kit form and assembled by the purchaser. Producers are no longer prepared to shoulder the financial risk of paying the huge levels of compensation that can be ordered by the courts if and when their planes crash.

By getting rid of this financial liability, producers have been able to sell their kits at very much lower prices, and this has had a powerful effect on sales. The skies are now full of planes that have been more or less assembled in people's garages. The singer John Denver was the first of many well-known figures to die in an aircraft that had been largely put together by himself.

In the world of Excelliance consumers are able to shop around at ease, and suppliers encourage them to do so. There is little to be gained from remaining loyal to a single supplier. So customers switch from one to another willy-nilly, aided by the fact that they have easy access to all the information that they need to enable them to make such a switch.

Nevertheless, consumers are very swayed by brand names.

So many purchases are now made electronically via the Internet and other forms of eCommerce that customers are increasingly detached from the goods and services that they want to buy. They cannot feel them or smell them. Despite the remarkable images transmitted on their high-definition television sets, they can only see what the supplier wants them to see. It is not like being in a shop, where what they see is what they get.

So consumers are turning to well-known brands and hoping that a quality name will provide some guarantee of a quality product. As a consequence, companies are investing heavily in brand names. But since those brands are increasingly global, they are having to promote their products' names right around the world.

That can be hugely expensive, and in order to make savings wherever they can companies have harmonised the names of their products. Many have taken the route followed some years ago by the Mars confectionery company. It changed the name of one of its most popular bars to Snickers in all its markets. (It had previously been known by a variety of names, including Marathon.)

One consequence of all this has been a large increase in the number of products known by an acronym—things such as HSBC financial services, BOC gases, and M&M confectionery. This avoids the difficult and expensive task of discovering whether a chosen brand name is acceptable in all markets. Exxon spent a fortune in order to find a single globally inoffensive word. But failing to find such a word can be expensive too. For example, the Irish Mist brand of liqueur has always had a hard time in German-speaking markets. In German, 'mist' means 'manure'.

Although producers have harmonised their products' appearance in most markets of the world, they have at the same time differentiated the products themselves. Procter & Gamble, for example, made an expensive mistake when it tried to globalise its washing powder. It soon discovered that cleaning clothes in one country can be a very different proposition from cleaning them in another. The hardness of the water differs, and so does the type of technology used and the local traditions. (Some people prefer to wash clothes in cold water, for instance.) So P&G has returned to making different powders for different markets... but it puts them all in identical packaging.

In other ways too today's demanding consumers are being fooled by appearances. Even when a product or service is associated with a single recognisable supplier, consumers are usually being served by a number of specialists at different points in the value chain. They may, for example, think that the pre-paid phone card that they are using has been provided by American Express (since that is the name on the outside of the card). But in practice their calls may be being booked with AT&T and their billing service being provided by yet another company. American Express is just a marketing front for the operation.

Normally customers don't realise that this has happened, but when they do they are not always happy about it. For example, a young French executive recently decided to boycott all products made by the Italian company Ferrari on the grounds that its corporate policy on the environment was irresponsible. She sold her Ferrari-designed car, and thought that was the end of it.

But then she went shopping just before Christmas and bought a new pen for her husband, a set of dining chairs for her younger brother's wedding, and a new bicycle for her sister. The very next day, however, she returned to the shop and angrily handed back the pen and the chairs. She had discovered from a friend in the meanwhile that they too had been designed by Ferrari.

This sort of arrangement has been in existence for many years now. People who bought an Aprilia motorbike or a Benetton pullover in the 1990s were not buying something that had actually been made by Aprilia or by Benetton. They were merely the front organisations that arranged for others to manufacture things that they then sold.

Markets

As the walls between industries fell in recent years, markets became overcrowded. New entrants poured into most sectors, and in many cases they were able to change the rules of the game in their particular market.

This has been largely due to technological change, but it has also been helped by the fact that many of them have chosen to be very focused. The Direct Line insurance business, for example, was not only a pioneer in telephone selling, it also insisted on selling only a narrow range of products to a narrow range of customers— essentially car insurance to statistically low-risk drivers.

The combination of these value propositions enabled Direct Line to undercut insurance premiums dramatically and to revolutionise the market. Time and again we have seen markets turned upside down by the interplay of rapid change in two or more different directions.

As globalisation has spread, markets that were traditionally the exclusive preserve of a handful of domestic firms have suddenly become open to foreign competition and to new ways of doing business. One of the earliest and most dramatic examples was that of the Japanese car industry. It was so successful in America and Europe in the 1980s, first with exports and then with foreign direct investment, that it revolutionised car manufacturing processes everywhere.

The speed with which that happened was determined to some extent by the time that it took for firms to set up distribution and servicing networks in foreign markets, and for them to supply goods as big and cumbersome as automobiles. As markets came to depend more and more on developments in information technology, however, that speed accelerated. The latest piece of software to come out of California's Silicon Valley is launched and marketed simultaneously around the globe. Delivered electronically to PCs, it does not need a world-wide distribution network. Nor does it take days at sea to get it to market.

The arrival of the Internet and of other forms of eCommerce has accelerated the process dramatically. New products launched and sold electronically in one market have found it difficult to limit their marketing effort. Demand comes, via the Internet and other on-line services, from all around the world simultaneously. Ever since the anti-impotency pill Viarga was launched in the late 1990s, drug companies have known that their new products will be instantly in demand all over the world.

Such is the pressure to get new products to market that regulators have been compelled to speed up their decision-making processes. And the regulators of most major industries in large industrialised economies have agreements among themselves that are designed to avoid time-wasting duplication. So a drug invented in the United States, once it has received the approval of the US's Food and Drug Administration (FDA), is free to be sold in most markets of the world.

Nowadays products are highly standardised. Ever since the Betamax and VHS systems tried to let the market decide on the standard for video recorders, firms have sought to establish uniform standards at an early stage in the development of new products.

Today's travellers recognise computers and other electronic equipment wherever they are in the world. It is not just the way that the product looks that is familiar; the way that it operates is also familiar. Switch on a PC in Djakarta and you go through exactly the same processes to access your home base as you did the previous week when you were in Duluth.

Car manufacturers' latest models are also highly standardised, and companies sell them in all markets of the world. Ford was one of the first to follow this route. Its early prototypes of a 'world car' (like the Escort and the Mondeo) often had wide variations—because of different national requirements on things such as the design of the headlamps or of the bumpers. But today the body and virtually all of the components in the major manufacturers' new models are the same—whatever market they are made for.

Industries

Products today are supplied by alliances of giant specialist firms, each of them occupying different positions on the value chain. The firms in these alliances have been forced to concentrate on a narrow range of core skills by the remorseless pressure for efficiency.

Industrial alliances come in all shapes and sizes. What they have in common is a shared understanding between the parties that together they can achieve something that individually and separately they cannot. They range from the loose relationship between a company and a preferred supplier to the binding legal agreements that may be required in a complicated franchise.

Alliances have been particularly popular in financial services. At the end of 1995 the average large American bank had 12 different alliances; by the end of 1996 that figure had risen to 30. By the end of the decade it had grown to several hundred.

Some alliances have brought together unlikely bedfellows. NatWest Markets, a British investment bank, has a joint venture with the UK Ministry of Defence to look into ways of using battlefield simulation technology to understand complex movements in the price of financial assets. And Yahoo!, an avant-garde on-line search engine, has a partnership with Visa

International, a traditional credit card company. The two firms provide a comprehensive on-line shopping guide.

One of the benefits of alliances has been in helping companies to reap new economies of scale. The industrial historian Alfred Chandler pointed out in the middle of the last century that the great American industrial fortunes of the early years of that century—those of families such as the Rockerfellers, the Paynes, and the Flaglers—'were all built on scale'. That insight fuelled a phenomenal growth in mergers and acquisitions. Firms sought to gain the advantages of scale first by buying other firms.

But then companies saw that they could tap into economies of scale much more cheaply by forming alliances. British Petroleum and Mobil, for example, claim that by folding their downstream European businesses into a joint venture they saved themselves $700 million a year. Other companies have found similarly innovative ways to make comparable savings.

Alliances have also been encouraged by the way in which the walls between different industries have fallen. All companies have been presented with a multitude of new commercial options. Traditional old-fashioned utilities, for example, have flirted with businesses as different as telecoms, retailing and financial services.

Faced with so many options, firms have looked for a way in which they can put a toe into new industrial waters before taking the full plunge. Alliances have provided them with a low-risk way to test new market opportunities. Often set up as low-profile separate operations, they can be closed (if they don't work) with a minimum of fuss and/or financial loss.

Alliances are also frequently used as a way to try out new geographical waters. Globalisation has encouraged all sorts of businesses to think of entering markets that used to lie far beyond their horizons. A relatively low-risk way for them to enter such markets is for them to link up with a local partner. National airlines, for example, have formed a number of alliances that allow them to offer services all around the globe. Typical is the link-up between American Airlines, China Airways and Qantas, now known as ACG. The vast majority of alliances involve partners from more than one nation.

Although alliances tend to be long-term relationships, they are sometimes disbanded for perfectly good market reasons. On occasions, disbanded partnerships have even been reformed at a later date. One prominent example is the alliance between Ford and Volkswagen.

In the mid-1980s Ford and Volkswagen formed a pioneering joint venture in Latin America. Called Autolatina, it pooled the two companies' loss-making operations in the region.

Before long, Autolatina succeeded in making profits in a highly volatile market where cars were being bought not just for transport but also as a hedge against inflation. A senior Ford executive said at the time that Autolatina was 'the surgical brace which saw Volkswagen and Ford through the difficult days of the South American auto market'.

Ten years later, when the economies of Latin America were far less volatile and government interference was less, the two companies decided that they wanted to return to running their own separate operations in the region. So Autolatina was dissolved at the end of 1995.

By the year 2002, however, Ford had narrowed its focus considerably and become a highly specialised manufacturing operation. Volkswagen, on the other hand, was by then a very sophisticated sales and distribution business, and particularly strong in Latin America. So the two companies decided to form a new bilateral joint venture which would give Volkswagen the right to sell Ford's cars exclusively throughout Latin America. The name of the joint venture, which is still operating to this day, is Autolatina.

Alliances have been formed on occasions for purely defensive reasons. One company set up a network of alliances after it was badly hit by recession. 'When we hit the wall,' explained a senior executive from the company, 'we realised that we couldn't continue to do everything ourselves. We needed to find ways to close our gaps, whether they be product gaps, service delivery gaps, or world class economics gaps. So we decided to go out in search of gap fillers through alliances and joint ventures, partnerships, handshakes—any way that made sense.'

Many firms have rushed to establish links with what they believe to be the only provider (or the only decent provider) of a particular technology or service. Some alliances have been consummated solely in order to prevent a firm's competitors at a particular point in the value chain from linking with powerful firms at other points in the chain. Many such alliances have proved to be like shotgun weddings: executed in haste and repented at leisure.

Nowadays it is possible to see a number of different patterns in these networks of alliances. There is, for example, the hub and spoke model. In this, a central capability (of marketing skills, say) is networked with the production and/or distribution skills of a number of other companies. The pattern is largely designed in order to help its participants to reap benefits of scale.

Then there is a type of alliance which enables a range of products and services (from a number of different producers) to be bundled together and brought to market as one. Yet another model is project-specific, bringing together a number of firms for one particular task. When the task is completed, the alliance is dissolved. This pattern has been familiar in the construction industry for many decades.

Undoubtedly the most popular pattern of network alliance today, however, is known as 'the value-chain venture'. This is designed to spread a capability on one particular point of the value chain to as wide a range of markets as possible. As companies become more and more focused on excelling at a core competence, they realise that they need to spread their excellence as widely as possible. To share in new pools of industrial value as and when they are discovered, they have to have alliances with those who have prior access to those pools. Hence a company like Netscape has formed alliances with a vast range of product and service providers in order to ensure that when they find new ways to satisfy consumer demands, it will be Netscape's software that they use to help them.

Firms cannot afford to wait until pools of value are discovered before setting out to take advantage of them. Those that do wait find either that the pool is dry by the time they arrive, or that competitor firms are ferociously guarding what dwindling puddles remain.

What some of today's market leaders are doing

The new style of global corporation was largely pioneered by the American car manufacturer Ford Motor. Troubled by shrinking margins in the automobile industry in the last years of the twentieth century, Ford commissioned a high-level internal study at the time to look into the company's future strategic options.

The study concluded that its margins were not likely to recover, due to 'traditional domestic competitors and a host of new entrants in the emerging markets that we have targeted for growth'. So Ford set about shedding most of its non-core businesses in a massive sale of the bulk of its assets.

The company then developed a five-year strategy designed to turn itself from an automobile corporation into a manufacturing powerhouse making products across a wide range of traditional industries. A few months later the company started making refrigerators for General Electric, and this soon proved so much more profitable than the automobile business that Ford began taking on other outsourced work.

Towards the end of the year 2002 the company announced another major reorganisation. This time it shed most of its marketing and design operations in order to concentrate even more on developing its core manufacturing business.

Two years later, Ford's chairman wrote a controversial book about the company's reorganisation. Called *Process Excellence*, it became a best seller and was all the rage with the gurus of change. In the book the chairman revealed: 'Our impetus to act was the undeniable realisation that there will be far too many of us competing for far too few resources.' (Ford IV, W.H., *Process Excellence: Surviving the Global Game*, New York: Houghton-Mifflin, 2004, p.17.)

Today Ford Manufacturing is nearing the end of a five-year transition period, and the company now assembles cars as well as other durable goods. These include appliances that were once made by Maytag and Whirlpool, companies that have abandoned manufacturing and that are themselves now successful design businesses.

Many of today's leading design firms have emerged from other areas. The Finnish company Nokia, for example, has been transformed from being one of the world's leading mobile phone manufacturers a decade ago into a consumer products design business today. In the first quarter of 1999, Nokia sold all its manufacturing operations to a rival, Philips Component Manufacturing. Now, six years later, the company is called Nokia Consumer Design Works. It co-operates closely with consumers, and co-designs with them a variety of consumer products. But it manufactures none of them.

Once a design is completed, Nokia passes it on to any number of specialist suppliers, manufacturers and shipping companies for production and delivery. Strict standardisation of technological specifications has enabled suppliers to compete on an equal basis no matter where they are—be they just down the road or at the other end of the earth.

Many other companies have moved into completely different businesses from those that preoccupied them in the 1990s. The heavily populated market for natural gas, for example, forced one major gas company in North America to become a provider of financial services.

In 2001 the company's losses were at an all-time high and there was no relief in sight. The only bright spots were a few investments that the company had made with money it had received from the sale of some infrastructure in geographical areas that it had deemed to be unprofitable.

These bright spots (and the imminent prospect of bankruptcy) focused the minds of the company's board of directors powerfully, and they took a bold decision to enter an entirely new line of business. In the middle of 2002 they began to sell off the company's assets, and what had not long before been a natural gas utility became a much smaller venture-capital firm.

Its core competence now is managing leveraged buy-outs and funding corporate start-ups.

In the Excelliance world, all suppliers are compelled to specialise in those activities at which they are best qualified. Some provide world-beating venture-capital services, others are leading distributors, product designers, product administrators, and so on.

AT&T, for example, was once America's leading telecommunications organisation and the world's biggest telephone company. But it grew tired of price wars in its industry, and of 'cherry picking' by upstart competitors. So in the year 2000 it abandoned the market for telecommunications services altogether.

Instead, AT&T decided to care for, maintain and upgrade its single largest asset (and its biggest core competence), namely a multi-billion dollar network infrastructure. The former AT&T is now known as Netco and is today concentrating on building up the world's number one broadband network, a network that is suitable for everything from phone calls to high bandwidth interactive multimedia. The phone calls and interactive multimedia are offered to consumers by third parties which have contracts with Netco to deliver the services over its network.

All sorts of products are now designed, manufactured, distributed and administered by third parties who have alliances with financial services marketing specialists. For over a decade now, for example, Barclays has been selling other people's cars as part of its car-loan service.

During that time Barclays Bank itself has been transformed. The company found itself ill-prepared at the turn of the century for the financial services market that was unfolding before it, and in the year 2003 market pressures forced it to split into a number of smaller companies. Each of these companies focuses on a particular core competence, and although each of them has been spun off and now operates autonomously, each still uses the Barclays name.

But that's about all that they share. So focused is Barclays Investment Management on its own profits for the coming year, for example, that it would just as soon use Virgin's authorisation systems as it would those of its sister company, Barclays' Transaction Processing. The marketplace dictates that each unit become the best-of-breed at all costs.

What it takes to succeed

In order to be successful in this scenario, corporations have had to combine truly excellent skills with far-sighted strategic alliances. It is not a world for the jack-of-all-trades; it is a world for the master of one.

Winners in the world of Excelliance have an innate ability to excel at one particular piece of the value chain; they are organisations that have demonstrated 'Process Excellence'. They do not have to be great marketers, but they do have to be good at building alliances and at focusing on what it is they do best. They do not find it easy to innovate outside their narrow sphere. Whenever they have been required to find new skills, they have done so by forming new alliances.

Today's successful firms also use information technology in a very particular way. Because only a small number of firms have actual 'face time' with clients, IT has thrived on helping companies with their back-office functions. Virtual workplace technologies, robust intranets, groupware, and collaboration support systems are the order of the day for the successful enterprises of the year 2008.

Winning firms are in effect 'outsourcing' everything except a very narrow range of activities to others who are more expert than they are. For example, few banks today process any of the transactions carried out by their customers, and few run their own call centres.

Companies such as First Data have become giants in a very narrow field. As long ago as 1995 First Data was processing up to 80% of all credit card transactions taking place in the United States. Today it is probably processing 80% of all credit card transactions taking place throughout the world. Over the years banks from Tennessee to Timbuktu have gradually agreed to fold their transaction processing businesses into joint ventures with First Data.

Outsourcing non-core activities to specialists has been done in two different ways: either competitively or collaboratively. General Motors pioneered the competitive route, and it keeps its suppliers on their toes through a series of short-term relationships that allow the giant car company to switch rapidly and frequently to the lowest cost provider. This style of outsourcing is often promoted as a way to reduce the opportunities for suppliers to become rivals.

Another car company, Chrysler, has pioneered the other (collaborative) way of outsourcing. It sets up longer-term partnerships with its suppliers and shares with them its know-how, personnel and financial risk. This system works very well when firms can identify the best suppliers and then lock them into exclusive agreements.

A key characteristic of successful companies today is excellence in managing the long- and short-term relationships that they have with their alliance partners and others. Alliances change over time, and they need to be managed over time.

Their management requires different skills from those that were needed when firms' operations were built on the old 'command and control' structure inherited from nineteenth-century military strategists. Such structures suited a business world in which companies were bought and sold, and where employees stayed with one employer for life.

In the new world of alliances, relationships between firms and their networks of partners are not based on ownership. They require a more consensual approach to decision making, more along the lines practised in the last century in Japan.

Today there are two main forms of alliance, and each of them requires a different style of management. On the one hand there is the bilateral relationship where the alliance is essentially between two organisations. And on the other hand there is the network alliance where an agreement to work together is made between three or more organisations.

Early examples of the former include the BP–Mobil joint venture already mentioned and the joint venture between Fuji, a Japanese photographic business, and Xerox, a pioneer in photocopying. Bilateral deals such as these are not normally very complex. And they usually have very clear aims which make their success easy to monitor.

Each party to the agreement generally has a well-defined contribution to make, so there is little opportunity for internal competition between them. Bilateral alliances are often able to run almost on autopilot, requiring little management effort on the part of either of the partners.

With networks of alliances it is a different story. They can be very complex, and in many cases there has to be a spider's web of agreements covering every combination of the partners. Early examples of complex networks like these were the Airbus consortium of European aircraft manufacturers and the Visa credit card franchise.

Networks of alliances also give rise sometimes to fierce competition between the partners, especially as and when they begin to smell success for their venture. Some networks fall apart when the partners find that their competing interests make it impossible for them to continue to work together.

In a number of cases networks have sloughed off members as their usefulness has ended, and taken on new ones to replace them. In a few instances alliances are being reformed almost continuously—one or two key partners and a central strategic aim being the only common thread throughout their life.

The bilateral type of alliance running on autopilot requires little more than a watching eye and some idea of strategic options should the deal go wrong. The network alliance, however, requires a much greater commitment of manpower. At one time this was thought to be a limitation on the size of any one network. Towards the end of the last century a senior executive at a major bank said of his organisation: 'in order to still be standing in five years, we are probably going to need 25 to 50 alliances, an unmanageable amount.'

What seemed an unmanageable amount a decade ago, however, is today commonplace. Not one of today's major financial institutions has fewer than 100 significant alliances.

For all its difficulties the network alliance is now the predominant form and bilateral deals are becoming less and less common. When they work well, network alliances bring rewards on an extraordinary scale. The potential synergy between the members of the alliance seems to increase geometrically in line with their number.

Winning firms say that the hardest thing about network alliances is gaining (and maintaining) everybody's commitment to the network. Over the years companies have learnt that there are two keys to keeping that commitment:

1   An effective initial structuring of the alliance. Individual firms need to consider from the very beginning how all parts of their organisation are going to be kept informed about the progress of the alliance. The parts also need to be trained to look for ways in which the alliance might be able to bring benefits specifically to them.

2   Cultural compatibility. Firms need to look for partners who are compatible. This can be as simple as picking on someone your own size. Large companies, for instance, find it easier to work with other large companies that have similar decision-making processes. A nippy little business that makes decisions rapidly (and that is looking for a rapid pay-back) may be frustrated working with a large traditional type of organisation.

Failure to get these two things right is far and away the commonest cause of the breakdown of alliances. Companies such as Hewlett Packard, Oracle and First Data were quick to create sophisticated structures for managing their alliances, and this enabled them to get a whole string of subsequent alliances rapidly into good working order.

Other firms have specifically gone out of their way to be seen as expert managers of their network alliances in order to improve their chances of being chosen to join the most desirable groupings of expert firms. Yet other firms, of course, have set themselves up as consultants in 'network alliance management'.

Early warning signs

The ways of this new business world did not spring up overnight. They evolved over a number of years. By the end of the last century it had already become very difficult for a single company to be all things to all people. An ever more global economy was even then placing an entirely new set of demands on companies and markets.

For those able to read them there were signs then to show which way things were going. During the 1990s, for example, companies were forming more and more alliances. The computer company IBM set up some 800 different alliances in the first half of that decade, and the prominent business leader Jack Welch, chairman of General Electric for over two decades, said at the beginning of the 1990s: 'If you think you can go it alone in today's global economy you are highly mistaken'.

Even at that time firms sometimes chose partners who were competitors in the same industry. In a landmark deal in 1996, for example, the American bank J.P. Morgan turned over the running of roughly one-third of its information technology activities to an organisation called the Pinnacle Alliance. The Pinnacle Alliance was a partnership consisting of Computer Sciences Corporation, Andersen Consulting, AT&T Solutions and Bell Atlantic Network Integration. The first two were fierce rivals in the IT field, the latter two in telecoms. Yet they worked together harmoniously in order to provide a truly excellent service for their client.

In another conspicuous case, an American financial institution called KeyCorp did what was then unthinkable and placed a picture of a competitor (Charles Schwab) on the cover of its annual report. The point of the picture was to announce a new alliance between the two firms. 'Competitors make powerful partners,' ran the caption.

This early rapid growth of alliances did not bring to an immediate end the era of mergers and acquisitions. Large deals were still being done in the mid-1990s—a record $500 billion-worth of mergers and acquisitions were announced in 1998 alone. In financial services, giants such as Chase bank merged with Chemical and Citibank merged with Travelers Group.

But by the turn of the century this activity had all but petered out. In the early years of this decade alliances became the main route for growth for companies right across the industrial spectrum.

Just as there were early signs of the subsequent popularity and shape of corporate alliances, so there were plenty of signs that leading companies were focusing on being excellent at a narrow range of business processes. The success of firms such as State Street Boston in financial services was a shining example to others.

More than half a century ago State Street began to shift from being a traditional full-service bank into becoming a specialist in back-office processing. Starting slowly, it offered its back office services to a number of other banks. As this business grew, State Street made a few acquisitions, and these increased the scale of its business and allowed it to keep investing in leading-edge technology. By the end of the century, the amount of money that relatively unknown State Street had under custody was 1.4 times the size of Germany's GDP.

Japan's economic crisis in the mid-1990s accelerated this

process of specialisation dramatically, and particularly in industries (such as automobile manufacturing) where Japan was at the time a market leader. Toyota had almost single-handedly given birth to the expression 'lean production' in the 1970s when it introduced a range of process improvements that enabled it to make a quantum leap in cost control and to leapfrog over its old-established western competitors. But by the mid-1990s Toyota and other Japanese manufacturers were under heavy pressure to become even leaner. Their markets in Europe and America were static because western manufacturers had responded so successfully to their first onslaught. And their local markets in Asia were drying up with the regional economic depression.

Toyota's rival Nissan cut its number of car platforms—the basic framework on which different car models are built—from 24 in 1995 to only five a decade later. At the same time it reduced its development times for new models from 19 months to 10 months. This cut costs by billions of yen a year and sharply tightened the focus of Nissan's production.

Nissan then joined other companies in responding to consumers' demands for more environmentally friendly cars. It rapidly restricted its production to vehicles with fuel-efficient engines, and it was a pioneer at the time in the development of what the company is now best known for—its hybrid vehicles running on a combination of batteries and a petrol engine.

Chapter summary

This chapter has explored the scenario we have called Excelliance in the year 2008. It is a scenario in which individual companies excel on a very narrow part of the value chain. In order to provide goods and services that meet the extremely high demands of consumers, they form alliances with large numbers of other firms which excel at other points along the value chain.

The chapter goes on to examine several famous companies and to see how radically they have changed in the previous decade (1998–2008). These companies include pioneers such as Ford, which is now exclusively a manufacturing operation, making goods under contract for companies such as General Electric. It also looks at Nokia, which was previously a manufacturer of mobile phones but which is now a designer of consumer products.

I then look at what it takes for a company to be successful in this scenario, and I focus on the need for skills to manage the complicated networks of alliances that are now at the heart of the world's best companies.

Finally I look back a few years and see how many early warning signs there were of the changes that were about to come. Anybody who had recognised those early warning signs would have been well placed to be a winner in the world of Excelliance.

8

Thunderstrike

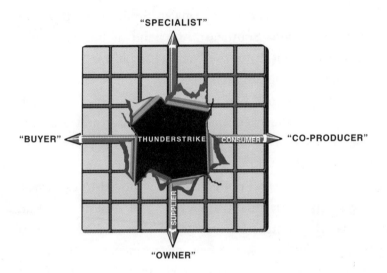

IN OUR FINAL SCENARIO I TRY TO IMAGINE THE WORST SITUATION
that industry and firms might have to live with—and the
emphasis is on the word 'live'. Anything worse and we are all
either scavenging animals or dead.

We call this scenario Thunderstrike, and in it, in the early
months of the year 2008, much of the world is at war. What
seemed like a minor incident in the Punjab seven years ago is now
totally out of control. Pakistan and India have been continually at

war ever since, and not long after the conflict began Bangladesh was inevitably drawn into the fighting too. Three of the world's ten most populous countries have now been engaged in a bloody war for longer than the duration of either of the great world wars of the twentieth century.

At the same time as the war in the Indian subcontinent widened, fierce battles began between a restless China and its neighbours in Korea and across the Taiwan Strait. This spread to disputed areas of remote Southeast Asia, and at one stage the fighting threatened to put the entire Pacific Rim at war.

In many areas the fighting has been continuous. But in some places there are occasional (if brief) periods of peace. At such times, companies in industries such as construction move in like vultures to get a piece of the action. Throughout the region there are no firms talking about thriving; only about surviving.

Everywhere politics and politicians have moved to extremes. Violent nationalists are rampant in Europe and America, and an ultra-nationalist government has just taken over in Russia. From St Petersburg to Vladivostok the new government is engaged in violent clashes with the terrorist mobs that have rampaged unchecked throughout the country for several years.

Elsewhere, fundamentalism has plunged fully one-third of Africa into civil war. Protests against Christian fundamentalist movements in parts of Mexico and South America have forced many companies to scale back or completely pull out of these markets as well.

The global economy is in chaos, and trade has broken down in many places. Inevitably investors have lost confidence in financial markets, and stock markets all over the world have not been so close to crashing for half a century. Trading on many exchanges is intermittent as market indices lurch violently up and down, but mostly down, and take them well beyond their permitted daily movements.

Investors have retrenched, as they do at such times, first into government bonds and then, as more and more governments have been forced to 'reschedule' their liabilities, into the traditional last resorts of the desperate saver: gold, precious metals and cash. Almost the only economy that is not in deep depression is South Africa; its geographical distance from the main theatres of war, and its ability to revive many of the gold mines that were closed as uneconomic at the end of the last century, has ensured that its citizens have continued to have a relatively decent standard of living. But even South Africans are severely restricted in what they can import.

Most trade now is carried out as barter. Currencies' exchange rates have become so volatile that traders prefer to exchange their production for other tangible products which they can then sell in local markets (and without taking any exchange rate risk). It is estimated that almost three-quarters of the world's trade is now in the form of barter, and over half of that is arms-for-food deals.

And this takes no account of the enormous black markets that have grown up at many border posts. At the border between Turkey and Iraq, for instance, vast unrecorded lorry loads of oil are exchanged every day for quantities of fruit and tea.

Nothing did more to upset trade in the West than Russia's attempted 'reclamation' of Finland in 2003. A force of 10,000 soldiers reached within 50 kilometres of Helsinki before pressure from Nato sent them back just in time to avert an all-out war. Nobody believes that this is the end of the story. The general feeling in the West is that the Russians came so close to success that, if it suits them, they will have another go.

Even without the presence of Russian troops on Finnish soil, Europeans that have a border with the former Soviet Union remain on edge. They are convinced that the new ultra-nationalist government in Russia is trying to destabilise their economies either by hard force or by gentle persuasion. Shooting across border fences by Russian soldiers is commonplace these days, and this prolongs the depression in the West by playing on the fears of consumers that there might be an invasion any day.

Under these circumstances, consumers are prepared to spend money on storing large quantities of sugar and flour. But they are not prepared to splash out on new cars, dishwashers or hats.

There have been a number of unidentified 'hackers' who have tried to corrupt vital defence systems on both sides of the fighting. And these hackers have not stopped at defence. They have also had a go at interfering with key monetary and financial systems. One fringe nationalist group in Russia, which is not represented in the current government, has admitted that one of its main aims is to undermine the financial system of the West by hacking into the inter-bank clearing. As far as we know, it has not yet succeeded.

With industries struggling to stay afloat, and with consumers increasingly angry at the rapidly deteriorating economic conditions, many governments are under pressure to create diversionary activities abroad. France has interned thousands of people of North African origin, claiming that they are playing out the conflicts of their home countries on the streets of Paris and other major French cities.

The United States government is also on the look-out for a foreign diversion. For many years it used intransigent Iraq as a scapegoat, wheeling out the Iraqi 'threat' whenever affairs got too hot at home. But the new right wing government in Washington has reverted to an even older scapegoat, harking back to the days of the 'Cold War' in the second half of the last century, when there was no more menacing threat to the farmers of the Mid-West than the Russian bear.

The idea of the Russian bear as a danger to the living standards of the average American has been resurrected. The

American media wastes no opportunity to insinuate that the Russians are plotting to undermine trade and the capitalist financial system. But these days it is an ultra-nationalist plot, not a communist one.

Many people think that it is only a matter of time before the United States and its NATO allies jump head first into war with Russia. They will find a diplomatic excuse, but their real reason will be to restore some semblance of order in one of their key markets and to secure access to vital raw materials.

Some go on to say that China will not be far behind. After invading Russia, the argument goes, the United States and its allies will have little choice but to move on into China, a far bigger market for all of them and also the source of some highly strategic raw materials.

Whether or not the allies decide to deploy their powerful armies in this way remains to be seen. But one thing is certain: the current volatile economic and political situation cannot be tolerated for much longer.

The perspective of consumers

All around the world the traditional 'consumer' has more or less disappeared and been replaced by what looks more like a 'survivor'. Established marketing categories no longer apply. For example, vast numbers of people have descended from middle-class comfort into a desperate scramble for survival. Many of those with real 'purchasing power' today are gangsters and black marketers whose demands differ greatly from those of traditional high net worth individuals.

What now exists is a world population living in increasing poverty. Those who have managed to escape poverty live in fear of the poverty they see around them. The number of beggars on the streets of major cities is increasing visibly all the time. In cities such as Moscow and Beijing it is now almost impossible to walk in public places without being assaulted. At night it is doubly impossible when the crumbling pavements become cluttered with cardboard boxes, makeshift blankets and sleeping bodies.

Even the once mighty North American economy has been hurt badly by the shutdown of global trade and the downturn of world markets. Consumer spending in the United States fell again sharply this year—it has now fallen by more than 20% since 2005 and there are few signs of a rebound. Computer sales have ground to a halt, and scarcely a week goes by without another microprocessor plant being shut down somewhere. The only bright spot in the electronics industry comes from the sales of computer security products. They are at an all-time high.

Sales of luxury goods have almost disappeared. Names such as Yves St Laurent, Louis Vuitton and Hermes have passed into history. Gucci, once an upmarket fashion and leather goods manufacturer, has managed to survive by diversifying into making military boots and belts. Its factories on the peaceful Mediterranean island of Sicily now manufacture most of the belts worn by soldiers on both sides of the conflict on the Indian subcontinent.

Those shops that do continue to cater to upmarket consumers have been forced to scale back their opening hours due to slow traffic in their stores. Harrods, London's most famous department store, has recently started to open only in the mornings. Since the Friday in July 2004 when Egyptian fundamentalists placed bombs that broke every single one of its windows, the store has anyway been open for only four days a week, from Monday to Thursday.

Abraham Maslow, an influential psychologist who died in 1970, has become a cult figure. Maslow was the first to attempt to rank individual consumers' needs, to define the higher level requirements which people seek to satisfy once their basic animal demands of food and shelter have been met.

Maslow's 'hierarchy of needs' put security and self-control at the top of the list—the things that people seek to satisfy before all others. This he followed with social relationships; self-esteem; status and recognition; achievement and challenge; power; creativity; and self-actualisation.

Today's consumers are sharply focused on satisfying their need for security and self-control. Electronic security devices are in great demand. People spend much of their time virtually under siege in their own homes. Home entertainment services and home delivery services are thriving. But restaurants and bars and other places where people used to meet and establish relationships have seen a sharp fall in business, especially those that relied on night-time trade.

People are very hungry for information. They want to know what is going on in other parts of the world in the hope that they can reassure themselves that disaster is not yet about to strike. Television news programmes are watched avidly and many people have become addicts of the growing number of news-only channels that are being broadcast around the world. However, a lot of these are spattered with government propaganda, so people are prepared to pay large sums of money for access to the few private-sector news services that they still trust.

Needs further down Maslow's hierarchy remain largely unsatisfied. In the Thunderstrike scenario there are few consumers in search of self-actualisation and creativity. Sales of books on yoga and gardening, two of the most popular pastimes in western society a decade ago, have plummeted. On the other hand, sales of books on martial arts and self-defence are enjoying a resurgence. Not since the early 1990s have they been so popular. Long-forgotten films by such masters of the martial arts, as Bruce Lee and Jackie Chan, have been revived and are now immensely popular all over the world.

Marketplaces

With much of the world at war, markets and marketplaces have changed dramatically. The desire for security has driven people off the streets. Old-fashioned 'shopping', in the sense of going into places called shops and buying things for cash, has been greatly reduced. Visits to shops are now very hurried affairs, and the last shop in New York to accept cash as a method of payment closed 12 months ago.

The growth of eCommerce has been stunted by people's fears that hackers can gain access to any electronic information anywhere. The World Wide Web, which a few short years ago promised to be a liberating influence on world markets, has instead become a tool for extremists of all kinds. It is also much used by underground terrorist groups, and has become an awkward mix of Radio Free Europe and hate propaganda.

The main technology driving markets is no longer information technology (IT). It is rather the technology of defence, and in particular of surveillance systems and of eavesdropping techniques, that is having the greatest impact on markets. Countries worried about the spread of war and unrest have been spending billions of dollars on developing new and ever more sophisticated early warning systems.

A wide range of commercial uses have been found for such technologies. Financial markets, for instance, use a number of sophisticated risk-management programs that were originally designed as part of military software. There are also a number of other products that have emerged from defence industry research which are now very popular consumer items. They range from heat-seeking sensors that can 'feel' through walls and are able to tell when any body (human or animal) comes within 500 metres, to pocket-sized remote-controlled video cameras that can take film at night. Both these items are now as common in well-to-do-homes as once were the letterbox and the doorbell.

It is not just private individuals who have become paranoid about security. Governments too are increasingly using technology to eavesdrop within their borders and to try and identify potential troublemakers. Commentators accuse them of becoming like 'Big Brother' in George Orwell's work of futuristic fiction, *1984*, written almost 40 years before that date. Orwell's nightmare scenario, they say, took a little longer to arrive. He should have called his book *2008*.

As governments become increasingly paranoid about the 'invisible enemy' in their midst, they are monitoring events with unprecedented vigour. This includes much greater supervision of markets and of changes in markets. Regulators are bigger and more powerful than they ever were, and the regulation of financial markets is particularly tight. Exchange controls have returned almost everywhere, and the international bond and debt markets have shrunk to next to nothing.

Everywhere markets have become strictly national, even in those countries still nominally at peace. The tendency for national regulators to combine their resources, so evident at the end of the last century, has been completely reversed. And anti-trust authorities no longer examine merger proposals for their monopoly implications; their sole aim is to find out if there are any foreign interests represented in either of the merging firms. For foreign shareholders are seen as potential fifth columnists for the political interests of hostile nations. National purity is the watchword of corporate life. Governments publish lists of the 'purest' firms and even give them special access to cheap loans.

This tide of nationalism has reversed the great fashion for globalisation and has pushed back the progress of standardisation. Countries now design products deliberately not to comply with other countries' standards—so that they cannot be used to help their war effort or, indeed, any preparation for war. This has dampened trade a great deal and adds to the difficulties of international travel.

Batteries, for instance, nowadays come in a number of different shapes and sizes, varying according to the country that produces them. This means that anybody taking an electronic gadget abroad is unlikely to be able to find replacement batteries should they be needed.

The biggest and most successful market these days is the black market. Twenty years ago it was estimated to account for 3–4% of the gross domestic product of western nations. Estimates, however, differed widely because of the difficulty in measuring something that, by definition, seeks not to be measured. For places such as Italy the figure was widely assumed to be higher.

Ten years later most estimates put the average figure at closer to 10%, and that was thought to be at the limit of what is acceptable. Yet today there are few nations where the black market does not count for more than half of GDP. In some countries that have been at war for a prolonged period the figure is reckoned to be even higher.

The perspective of suppliers

The structure of most industries that are not defence related is now chaotic. Like consumers, they are in the business of survival. Few have strategic plans that involve growth, so the massive activity in mergers and acquisitions and strategic alliances, that was such a feature of the last years of the twentieth century and the first years of this, has come to an almost complete standstill. The barbarians are no longer at the gate; they are inside the corporate walls, and they are scavenging for business.

Strategic alliances, which once held out such promise for

growth, are being disbanded even more quickly than they were originally put together. The Swiss Bank, the biggest bank in the world, had fewer than ten strategic alliances in 1990, more than 40 by 1998, and 220 by 2002. Today it has one.

In their haste to extricate themselves from international alliances, many companies failed to follow the letter of their agreements. This led to a host of cross-border legal actions, all of which will have to be cleared up before there can be a return to the levels of international trade seen in the past.

The power of Asian industry, that once seemed such a threat to the west, has now been tamed. Countries such as Malaysia, Thailand, Indonesia and the Philippines, which 15 years ago seemed full of promise, had a brief setback in 1998 when their economies were reined in by some over-exuberant lending. On that occasion, however, the countries learnt from their mistakes very quickly, and by the beginning of the new millennium their economies had bounced back.

Today, however, these countries look back on 1998 as a golden year. Intermittent warfare throughout the region has forced most industries there to close, and the local populations have been reduced to subsistence living.

In the mid-1990s many western companies geared themselves up to become global operations, and as part of this exercise they invested large sums throughout Asia. But in recent years they have found their local operations to be massively overstaffed. Declining demand in the region has gradually forced them to lay off large numbers of local employees.

This led to a famous incident in 2006. Many of the pharmaceuticals companies had taken advantage of low wage costs to shift production to South East Asia which became something of a global centre for drug production. However, the decling economy and rising global tension led to these firms not only cutting staff but moving production back to the safety of the home market. The effects on local economies were devastating. 'Pharmacon Valley' outside Bangkok had once been home to a thriving collection of manufacturing plants, R&D centres and regional headquarters for the major pharmaceutical companies. By 2006 all that was left was one giant production plant, mass producing contraceptive pills and agricultural hormones for the region. When this closed with the loss of 10,000 jobs it led to a riot. The furious ex-employees, with no prospect of another job, sacked the plant and drove away with hundreds of millions of dollars worth of pharmaceuticals which they proceeded to dump into the waters of Bangkok harbour. The incident has come to be known as the Bangkok Pill Party. Two years later many species of fish had still not returned to the upper reaches of the Gulf of Siam.

Many companies have found their overseas assets either stranded or abandoned. The pharmaceutical factory in Bangkok, for instance, is now just a rusting shell. The remaining employees were laid off within six months of the Bangkok Pill Party, and the building has been used by at least two guerrilla groups as a temporary headquarters.

Throughout the region there are vast areas of industrial wasteland where factories, warehouses, cranes and derricks have been left to rot. Tall tower blocks that once housed the offices of proud multinationals have been taken over by squatters who aggressively defend their right to be there. In some instances squatters have used force to occupy offices that had not yet been closed by their foreign owners.

Firms have gained a stronger foothold in their home markets because of the (often enforced) withdrawal of foreign competitors. But in all sectors other than those related to defence and security, markets are saturated and firms are at best having to paddle hard in order to stay still. All of them have had to learn to live with the black market, which involves turning a blind eye to some of its less savoury practices. As a subject, business ethics has fallen completely off the corporate agenda.

And with it has disappeared corporate concern for the environment. Companies are returning to the cheaper and more polluting fuels that they used before the environmental movement persuaded them to switch to cleaner sources of energy. Heavy smogs have returned to London for the first time in 50 years.

So fierce is the competition in their saturated domestic markets that companies are cutting corners wherever they can. Child labour has returned in many industries. But governments are afraid to take action because they realise that the cost of the war effort will go up if they insist that industry use fully paid adult labour. There are many children working in explosives and military electronics factories.

The growth of the black market has had a dramatic effect on government revenues. Revenues from VAT in the UK, for instance, fell by 45% in the year 2007. All governments are having to make their budgets stretch as far as possible—especially their defence expenditure. Some have sought to make ends meet by printing money, but that has led to hyperinflation in places like Myanmar and Somalia.

The temptations offered by persistant global conflict proved too much for many companies in their efforts to maintain sales and turnover. Clandestine supplies to 'rebels' provided a quick and dirty remedy to short-term balance sheet problems, and were easily hidden from overstretched government agencies.

However, once media investigations into terrorist atrocities, particularly in the bloody Sri Lankan conflict, revealed the depth of involvement of some major Western firms, public revulsion was such that one or two previously household names quickly declined into bankruptcy.

In most sectors firms have cut back drastically on their R&D. Innovation in technology has stalled and there has not been a major new operating system for PCs since Windows 02. Intel's promise in the late 1990s that the memory of its chips would soon double at no extra cost has proved hollow. Intel's chips are no more advanced today than they were at the turn of the century.

What Ford and others are up to

Individual firms have reacted very differently to the violent changes in their circumstances, and some were compelled to act more swiftly than others. The Ford Motor Company, for example, had to pull out of most of its non-western markets at the turn of the century. Religious fundamentalist movements that were spreading right across Africa and Asia, from the Bosphorus down to Cape Town and as far as the Great Wall of China, were demanding not only that women should not drive, but that they should not even leave their homes. This had a very direct effect on the demand for automobiles.

The automobile market deteriorated further with the wars that followed. Sparked by decades of border disputes, the fighting that had started in the Indian subcontinent spread rapidly across much of Africa, Central Asia and the former Soviet Union. The demand for cars plummeted when the men in these countries headed for the battlefield. The women they left behind walked when they had to, but for the most part they stayed indoors. Cities such as Cairo and Nairobi, which had become choked with traffic and pedestrians, were suddenly silent.

Ford, like many other companies with a world-wide operation, found itself with far too much inventory and excess capacity for the saturated western markets which became its main focus. Realising early on that the defence industry was a business to be in, it looked for ways to realign itself towards military transport. To do that in any reasonable time span, however, it needed to find a partner.

For a while Ford contemplated a merger with Raytheon, which is today the world's largest corporation in terms both of sales and of market capitalisation, having taken over that mantle from Microsoft three years ago. In the last century Raytheon was responsible for some of the most breathtaking commercial inventions. It developed the first guided missiles, for instance, and it adapted World War Two radar technology to invent the microwave oven.

But despite being a global organisation with a multi-billion dollar turnover and an extraordinary track record for invention, Raytheon fell out of favour in the 1990s. Governments decided that the end of the Cold War, the stand-off between the United States and the Soviet Union, meant that they could cut back on defence expenditure. It was only in the early years of this century that Raytheon began to hit the public eye. In 2002 it became the hottest stock in the world, with the rise in its share price almost exactly mirroring the fall of the New York stock market's main index.

The merger talks with Ford, however, fell through. There was bitter disagreement over the financial terms of a deal, and the scope for synergy did not at the end of the day seem to be all that great. Raytheon was keen to develop its high-resolution satellite imaging technology. Not only was this in great demand from governments and the private sector for surveillance activities of one sort or another, but it could also be used to detect underground resources such as oil and other minerals.

As countries were forced to become more and more self-sufficient they were eager to find and exploit any natural resources that did not have to be imported. One of Raytheon's biggest businesses is hunting for underground water. With the widespread breakdown in public services, more and more households are looking to find their own water and to build their own wells.

Ford on the other hand was keen to diversify into military

vehicles, a more natural development from its existing business. And so the company eventually formed an alliance with British Aerospace. British Aerospace is a defence-related company like Raytheon, but it has not been nearly so successful in recent years.

The venture with Ford is unusual in that it is between companies of different nationalities. But so strong was the North Atlantic alliance at the time that the US authorities allowed companies to form ventures with foreign partners from only two countries in the world—the UK and Canada.

Ford is now planning to convert half of its US automobile factories into defence-related manufacturing plants. The plan is that the joint venture (called Ford Aerospace) will manufacture radar, tanks and other defence equipment. The company has said that it anticipates that the venture will enable it to declare a small profit for the year 2010. If it does (and the company has little on which to base its financial projections) it will have turned round a ten-year downward trend.

Barclays' recent history indicates more clearly what it takes to be successful in the Thunderstrike scenario. At the beginning of the century it and the other banks faced a major problem which first came to light in 2002. That year a revealing Bank of England report was obtained by the press. The report contained details of the ways in which the various banks proposed to counter illegal computer hacking, and it contained a number that the media turned into a sensation. Computer hacking, it said, had caused losses of more than $1 billion in the previous three years. And the amount was rising by almost 50% a year.

The general public, still extremely nervous about entrusting the transfer of their assets to electronic means, deserted the banks in droves. The public began to keep its savings in the form of gold and other precious metals. The price of gold soared to more than $1,000 an ounce and the demand for safes that could be hidden in walls at home grew astronomically.

Anxious to restore public confidence in its electronic services, Barclays began one of the most ambitious computer security programmes in industrial history. After a year spent developing and tailoring some of the most expert systems on the market, Barclays launched its 'hacker-proof' service. A sceptical public was slow to return to traditional banking, but Barclays was gradually able to convince its former customers that it had a genuinely secure system.

This process was assisted by the fact that the bank began to sell its system to other financial institutions. Indeed, so successful did it become that 'hacker-proofing' is now for Barclays a profitable business in its own right. It is also a growing business. The company is beginning to license the system's protocol to airlines and to telecommunications companies.

But Barclays' success in restoring confidence in the financial system has been limited. Its overseas operations are far more restricted than they used to be, and its success in selling 'hacker-proofing' abroad has been less than the bank had hoped for. Many countries are suspicious of any foreign involvement in their monetary or financial systems.

In such places there is still not a lot of trust in financial institutions. Although the price of gold has fallen back slightly over the past year, it remains at historically high levels. All over the world gold coins and bracelets are used as stores of value. The US dollar is favoured wherever people can get hold of it, and one or two new currencies have joined the select few 'hard' currencies that have been trusted by savers for decades—the Argentinean peso, for instance.

Today Barclays knows that its opportunities abroad are limited. For other companies and other industries, however, there are still a number of interesting opportunities in far-flung parts of the world. But the risks involved in seizing them are greater than ever.

Take a company like British Gas. The growth of terrorism around the world has put its assets at very high risk and created enormous problems for the company. Nevertheless it is still seeking new business and is courting a number of governments in the hope of winning some of the big contracts that are about to be awarded as part of the major reconstruction of large chunks of the Pacific Rim.

British Gas is spending lots of money on regional lobbying efforts, and its executives are engaged in a constant effort to get close to governments and political bodies in the region. This is far more of a problem than it used to be ten years ago. In the first place, politicians die (or just disappear) with far greater frequency. Western businessmen have found themselves returning home with a contract signed by a key minister only to find on their return that he has been ousted by a group prepared to renege on all their predecessors' promises.

Doing deals in Asia has also been made more difficult by the problems of travelling round the region. In many areas flights have been stopped because air transport is too dangerous. In 2005 a 'jumbo' jet was shot down over Papua New Guinea by a then unheard of terrorist group which, it eventually transpired, had no more than a dozen committed members. The primitive rocket launcher that the group had taken into a remote part of the jungle in order to shoot down the plane had cost no more than a few hundred dollars.

On top of the terrorist threat, economic depression in the region has also curtailed scheduled flights dramatically. The result is that British Gas's executives have to spend long periods of time (months on occasions) at 'the front line', holed up in spartan hotels close to ministerial offices and never very far from a war zone. The company's own fleet of converted fighter planes ferries them back and forth from one troubled capital to another. A seasoned salesman with the company has compared it to the

situation in Moscow immediately after the fall of the last
communist government there—with one qualification. Today it's
ten times worse.

The rewards for all this effort, however, can be considerable.
The recent truce between China and the Philippines has resulted
in a number of large infrastructure contracts going to overseas
bidders. British Gas itself managed to win an $875 million
contract to rebuild and modernise Manila's bombed out natural
gas pipelines. The company has refused to reveal what profit
margin it expects on the deal, except to say that it is
'commensurate with the considerable risk involved'.

Others have not fared so well in the region. British Telecom,
for example, finds that the infrastructure that it set up with a
number of different business partners in various parts of Asia is
continually coming under terrorist attack. These attacks take place
both on the ground—through the use of explosives—and in the
air—through the use of electronic viruses and such like.

Maintaining this network is proving enormously expensive
and the company has been forced to renegotiate the terms of a
number of contracts. To add to its troubles, there is a growing
demand from corporate and governmental clients in the region for
guaranteed high levels of data protection. In order to provide this,
the company has been compelled to make massive investments in
security systems.

When BT does not make the investment it simply loses the
business. Nobody in the region wants to use old-fashioned
unsecured electronic links; it's safer today to use pigeons.

BT, and many of the world's PTTs, began the decade still
riding the wave of deregulation. Now, with formerly promising
markets in Asia and Africa under siege, and traditional markets in
Europe and North America virtually saturated, national PTTs are
looking to their governments for help.

The help they seek is neither novel nor high-tech; in fact it's as old as the hills—namely, protection for its home market. The British parliament is expected to pass a bill in the next few months that will almost totally eliminate foreign access to the UK's telecoms markets.

Governments in continental Europe and North America are already drafting tit-for-tat legislation, happy that they were not the first to move, but happy too for the chance to relieve the pressure that they have been under from their own national firms. It will not be long before the telecoms industry has returned to the bad old (pre-deregulation) days of the early 1980s.

There is not much to stop it any more. The European Commission, which used to be such a powerful influence in opening up individual EU markets to competition (and ensuring that they remained open) is now a spent force in industrial matters. It has made no effort to stop any of the spate of anti-competitive alliances and mergers that have been taking place between some of Europe's largest firms, and it has failed to exert any influence on the British government in the drafting of its new protectionist law on access to the telecoms market.

There is no special treatment in the British legislation even for firms based within the European Union. French telecoms service providers will have as little opportunity to do business in the UK as those from Malaysia. The bill's supporters have argued that the European Union is now so large that if the bill were to give special treatment to firms from within the EU, it would include such a large percentage of the world's major players that the legislation would be totally ineffective in providing British Telecom with what the bill's drafters have called 'temporary protection' until markets return to 'a reasonable degree of normalcy'. The drafters have not attempted to define what is to constitute 'a reasonable degree of normalcy'.

The European Commission has been handicapped in recent years by a severe shortage of staff. Although there is no major war currently being waged within the borders of the EU, the Brussels-based organisation has found that its extensive foreign interests have made it a prime target for terrorists.

The exodus of staff began soon after the shooting of the German commissioner for the environment. He was gunned down with his wife and children as they waited in their Mercedes Benz at a traffic light on the Avenue Louise. Nobody was ever charged with the crime, but the word on the Internet was that it was the work of a group of environmentalists who were objecting to the building of a munitions factory by a German consortium on 'protected' land outside the Brazilian city of Manaus.

Many of the Commission's staff left in order to return to the relative safety of their own countries. Those that remain have become very security conscious. Gone are the days when Brussels bureaucrats rode around in ostentatious cars. Their upmarket Jaguars and BMWs first became a prime target for the Russian Mafia, whipped away to an east European garage before they had even been reported as missing. Subsequently, and more seriously, they became easy prey for every grenade-toting terrorist in town.

Today, the dwindling number of bureaucrats who continue to brave Brussels' terrorist-infested streets make every effort to remain as inconspicuous as possible. If they drive a car at all it is as likely to be a ten-year-old beaten up Ford Ka as it is to be a new reinforced and bullet-proof limousine.

Early warning signs

The early warning signs for the Thunderstrike scenario were significantly different from those for the other four scenarios. For they were to be found largely in the political rather than the industrial and commercial arena. Some lay in deep-seated social changes that ultimately brought about political change: the fundamentalist movement, for instance, whose earliest signs can be traced as far back as the overthrow of the Shah of Iran in 1979.

The movement gradually gathered steam thereafter, first in Egypt and Algiers and then in all parts of the Muslim world. Its impact was soon felt throughout the Christian world as Muslim communities there grew more confident in asserting their religious beliefs, and as Muslims everywhere became more insistent that products and services be produced according to Muslim principles. For example, Islamic banking, in which the payment of interest is forbidden, spread quickly, and western banks found themselves unable to offer a competitive service. Their markets shrank throughout the Muslim world.

Outside the Muslim world there were other signs that societies were growing increasingly restless and more prepared to take extreme measures to attain their ends. Slower than expected economic progress in China was followed by very aggressive behaviour towards its neighbours and other countries in the region. China annexed North Korea in 2003, South Korea in 2004 and Taiwan in 2005. At one time there was scarcely a nation between Myanmar and Australia that was not involved in some internal ferment that had been sparked off by its expatriate Chinese community.

At first the Chinese conflicts had little impact on western markets. The Chinese had not yet become the consumers that western producers had been hoping for. They were still largely a society of bicycling peasants. But once they invaded South Korea and Taiwan and disrupted the economies of other advanced Asian nations, the rest of the industrial world began to feel the impact.

Another major political change that flashed warning lights for the future of the world economy was the failure of the former Soviet bloc nations to create viable market-oriented democracies, a failure that became only gradually apparent. For a while there was a resurgence of communism in these countries, largely as a reaction to the appalling maldistribution of wealth that followed the first opening up of the Soviet bloc economies.

This has been followed by a nationalist counter-reaction, and Russia is now ruled by an ultra-nationalist government that is pre-occupied with fighting countless communist guerrilla groups throughout the countryside. Both political factions are allied with like-minded groups in the other countries of the former Soviet bloc, so the conflict in Russia is mirrored everywhere from Warsaw to Alma Ata.

Chapter summary

In this chapter I have gone outside the parameters that shaped the previous four, and have tried to imagine a 'wild card' scenario in which large parts of the world are at war. As we drew out the other scenarios it became increasingly apparent to us that there is a possibility that the two most important changes that we had identified (and that we considered, at their extremes, in those scenarios) could be rendered insignificant by social unrest and widespread warfare.

Under this scenario, called Thunderstrike, the world economy is in chaos and politicians have swung violently in favour of nationalism. An ultra-nationalist government has just taken over in Russia. Consumers are not recognisable as such any more. Their main concern is safety, and the sales of security devices are booming. In countries still at peace most people have become prisoners in their own homes.

They are afraid to go to shops, and many shops are closing for part of the day. But consumers still don't trust eCommerce. So buying and selling is done mostly over the telephone.

Markets and prices are highly volatile. There is hyperinflation in a number of countries and stock markets are frequently closed because of erratic price movements.

The chapter goes on to consider a number of well-known companies and to suggest ways in which they might have survived under this scenario. In general, companies that succeed are either in defence and defence-related industries. (The Ford Motor Company, we suggest, will survive because of an alliance with British Aerospace.) Or they have a very tight focus on the needs of people who live in an almost continual state of fear. (Barclays, for example, will be making much of its profit from supplying other firms with its own excellent system for ensuring that computer networks are 'hacker-proof'.)

Finally I look back and see what early warning signs there were of the changes that were about to come. In this scenario most of the early warning signs were political not commercial. Anybody who recognised them could not reasonably have expected to thrive under the Thunderstrike scenario; the best they could have hoped for would have been survival.

PRESENT DAY

9

Insights for all industries

L ET'S NOW RETURN FROM OUR JOURNEYS INTO THE FUTURE and come back to the present day.

It is my hope that reading Chapters 4 to 8 has at least made you feel uncomfortable, and undermined some of the assumptions and 'certainties' on which you have so far based your future planning. If it has, however, it is not the intention of this book to leave you feeling that the floor is disappearing beneath your feet. For my message is a positive one. There may be no certainties in this world except death, taxes and change, but there are a number of things that we can do now to help prepare for future uncertainty. Doing these things will help restore some more solid foundations to the business world.

First, of course, you can do some scenario planning for yourself. But, since we now know that each scenario demands a very different strategy, does that not imply there is nothing we can do strategically in the meanwhile until we have fleshed out our own scenarios?

The answer is a very definite 'no'. There are a number of strategic moves which companies are relatively safe in taking regardless of which scenario eventually unfolds. These 'robust strategies' or 'no-brainers', which apply in all circumstances, can be roughly divided into five:

✦ In the first instance, companies need to stay flexible. There are two aspects to this: one is for them to slim down; the other is for them to become more nimble.

✦ Secondly, companies need to keep trying things out; they need to keep 'getting wet' and to be learning continually from that experience.

✦ Then they need to gain a thorough understanding of their core competencies. Only that way can they hope to learn how these can be leveraged in order to take rapid advantage of any new opportunities.

✦ Fourthly, companies need to keep monitoring the business environment around the globe so that they can quickly take on board significant shifts and think through the implications for them.

✦ And finally, companies need to keep on introducing insights from outside in order to refresh their thinking and to ensure that they are not so blinkered that they totally fail to see what's catching up behind them.

In the pages that follow I will expand briefly on each of these five robust strategies. I am sure that you will recognise, however, that it will take more than a single chapter or even a single book to cover these strategies in sufficient detail.

Stay flexible

It is fundamental that in a world of rapid change firms need to remain as flexible as possible. Only that way can they hope to move rapidly in whichever direction they see change occurring. Part of the technique lies in remaining financially liquid so that funds are always available to make the big move at the moment when a firm wants to lock itself into a particular scenario.

For large established firms, anything beyond that is not easy. A big UK bank, for instance, is a bit like an oil tanker. There is no way that it can turn on a sixpence. It has to live with the huge branch network and the legacy computer systems that have been developed over the years to support its operations. But any big established firm should be asking itself whether it really needs to be so big. Because the slimmer you are, the faster you can turn.

One way to slim down is by outsourcing.

You might ask do big banks really want to employ thousands of people to key in to their computers the details of every single cheque, for example? There's not much competitive advantage to be gained there. Indeed, this was just the conclusion that some US bankers from five different banks came to one evening while having dinner together. Over coffee one of their number wondered how many cheques they were able to process in total. They concluded that between them, they could probably process all the cheques in the US! That night a new company was born to process the cheques of those five banks. These banks committed to handing all of their cheque processing to this new 'shared services company' as well as a portion of their current cheque-handling staff. The banks concerned are now spending a lot less on cheque processing and are able to concentrate on the more important, core parts of their business.

In fact the five owning banks did one other interesting thing. They told some other banks what they were doing suggesting that they also set up such a shared service themselves. You might ask why these five banks did not try to convince the other banks they approached to use their new shared service. Well, they wanted these other banks to set up a competitive venture to their own so that their venture would be kept on its toes!

The huge oil company BP has made itself more flexible by outsourcing a vast range of operations that it does not consider to be central to its business (including its accounting function, which it outsourced to Andersen Consulting). Much of BP's Wytch Farm oil-drilling operation in the south of England—from the receptionist to the actual drilling—is outsourced to others. BP says that its business there is 'environmental management', one of its core competencies, not providing receptionist services nor even drilling.

So big businesses can get slimmer. And once they're slimmer it's easier for them to become more nimble. Nimbleness can also be achieved by flattening an organisation, shedding layers of non value-added management and getting closer to the things that matter, and especially customers. I asked one chief executive with wide industrial experience soon after he moved into the top job at a very large financial institution, what it was like. 'It's so high,' he said, 'I can't see the bottom'. He soon set about creating a more nimble, less lofty organisation.

In most companies, I have found that the technology and processes have more often been developed to suit the management structure than the customer. Thus you will often find systems that were designed for individual departments to allow them to monitor their performance and just their products and services rather than an integrated set of systems available to all personnel which allow all personnel to assess the performance of the whole company and to also obtain information on specific customers or suppliers no matter how they are served. Companies need to restructure themselves for greater flexibility with this thought in mind.

Another way to become more nimble is to create special teams 'to manage change'. A common problem in organisations today is that they view change as an occasional intrusion into everyday life, something that has to be taken on board by people who already have full-time jobs. Change management will only get the attention it deserves when special teams are set up to handle it rather than have operational management do this as well as their day jobs.

Get wet

Perhaps the most important thing that companies can do today—regardless of their markets or how they evolve—is to keep on trying new things and new ideas. Identify a broad range of business possibilities for the future, and then go and try them out. And try them properly. It is no good, as it might have been in the old days, to 'put a toe in the water'. That is only a half-hearted commitment that doesn't teach the owner of the toe much about the water.

Nowadays firms need to get thoroughly wet (from head to toe) in all sorts of new things all the time. They need to improvise, to learn on the hoof as it were, in order to understand properly how any new business works. Banks, for instance, are today only just beginning to immerse themselves in the possibilities of the Internet. When the technology of the Internet first became available, all that they could do was put up a page on the Web and invite customers to seek further information. When queries did come in electronically, many banks had not invested in the means to respond to them. It was worse even than putting a toe in the water.

At last, many banks have realised that this is not enough. They need to offer full Internet services to customers in order to find out how such a system operates. It may not make them money—at the moment there are only a few hundreds of thousands of customers using Internet banking in the UK. But what if it were suddenly to take off? Banks that have run a fully working pilot scheme will then be well placed to take advantage of the moment. If it doesn't take off, of course, they have lost all the investment that they put in. But the wise ones will know that it was an investment that they could not afford not to make.

The cost of not getting 'wet' can be considerable. Look, for example, at what happened in the UK with telephone banking. When it was first begun—by a company called First Direct—the traditional high street banks 'pooh-poohed' it, saying that customers would always want the face-to-face service that could only be provided through a branch network. Without ever having tried it, they were convinced that telephone banking was going to fail.

When it didn't, and when First Direct started to make significant inroads into the top end of their customer base, the high street banks belatedly decided that they had to respond. They had to offer their customers a telephone banking service, and they had to do it quickly and without having had a chance to think it through very carefully.

As a consequence, what most banks created was an expensive appendage to their existing arrangements, ones that were not suited to subsequent integration or expansion.

Companies must keep trying all sorts of new technologies, many of which will not turn out to be the wave of the future. And if that seems difficult, try setting up a special 'innovation unit' whose only job is to try new things. And encourage them to be free thinkers; let them not have to wear suits and ties in the office.

My job at Andersen Consulting is essentially to lead just such a group. For we want to help our clients to be in a position when something really does take off in their industry (and these days that can happen with extraordinary speed—whether it be the market for male anti-impotency pills or for BMX bikes) that it does not come at them from 'a point of surprise', from that blind spot which their wing mirrors don't cover.

All this means that organisations must be prepared to fail a lot of the time, and that they must learn how to learn from that failure. This goes against the grain and is something that many corporate cultures find hard to take on board. A few, like the venture capital outfit 3i, acknowledge that failure is part of their life. Seven out of every ten ventures that 3i backs fail yet the three that succeed more than cover the cost of the other seven; they make 3i a healthy profit. But other organisations, nervous about public attitudes to failure, prefer not to use the 'f' word.

On the other hand, there are a few organisations that

specifically set out to put their high fliers into divisions that they suspect will fail in order to give them the chance to learn from the experience. The ubiquitous Virgin, which does not make a success of everything that it tries, gives those people charged with coming up with ideas for new business ventures three-monthly targets. If they are not met, the idea is dropped, and nobody talks about failure.

Some other companies, when recruiting for their top management echelons, look specifically for people who have known what it is to fail in business. It is said that the fact that Marjorie Scardino had run a newspaper business in America that had failed was instrumental in persuading Pearson plc that she should be the first woman ever to run the British media group—and indeed the first woman ever to run a company that is a constituent of the FTSE100, the UK's major stock market index.

Understand core competencies

Another general step that companies can take regardless of the scenarios that they outline is to determine their core competencies. What is it that they do that is at the heart of their business? What is the core competence of a big bank, for instance? Could it be secured money transmission or risk management? As you read earlier, US bankers do not think it is cheque processing.

Once a firm has decided what its core competencies are, it can start to shed those areas which fall outside them or seek to offer those core competencies to other firms. It might want to shed a process, a subsidiary, or even a distribution channel, or offer to provide financial products to a retailer wanting to enter financial services, for example.

In order to fill the gaps that this will inevitably leave, the firm then needs to set about forming alliances with outside partners. But forming successful alliances is not easy; their history is scattered with expensive failures—think about Olivetti and AT&T, or Tesco and NatWest, who fell out when NatWest realised that it was basically encouraging a rival to steal its customers and its market share. Firms need to have a go at forming alliances at the earliest opportunity. They need to 'get wet' trying out one or two.

Some of the most successful firms at forming alliances are the big retailers, for they have had valuable experience in what it takes to get them right. When a customer complains about a bad tomato that they have bought at Sainsbury's, say, they complain to the big UK retailer just as if Sainsbury had grown the tomato itself. But, of course, Sainsbury doesn't actually manufacture anything itself—not even the boxes in which the tomatoes are transported, never mind the tomatoes themselves.

So any retailer is highly motivated to establish a relationship with its suppliers (of tomatoes and of everything else) which ensures that the goods they supply are of a quality to which the retailer wants to attach its reputation. The bond that this entails between retailer and supplier is just what is needed to make a good alliance work.

Banks, by and large, are of a totally opposite complexion. They do everything for themselves—they clear their own cheques, run their own call centres, and keep their own cash. In a specialist world they may find themselves vulnerable because they have so little experience of forming alliances. So a wise bank today will be trying out alliances in a number of different directions—for example, by selling somebody else's products.

A number of forward-looking financial institutions are indeed doing just that. In South Africa, for example, Liberty Life took a close look at the 15 or so different main products that it was selling and asked itself in which of them it was 'best of breed'. Its answer was, 'only a handful'.

So the company turned to those competitors whom it considered were producing superior products and said to them,

'We'll sell your products under our brand name and, at the same time, we'll stop selling our competing (but inferior) products'. The strategy was highly successful, improving the company's profits considerably in a short space of time. But it was not effected, of course, without some pain.

Continuous monitoring

Another thing that all companies can do is to develop listening devices, early warning systems that provide them with information on what's happening in the outside world that might have a bearing on their business. In today's world of information overload, the key here is to devise systems that help to retrieve and collect relevant data quickly. This involves things such as the sophisticated use of keywords when searching for information from on-line service providers, and making use of 'push technologies'—technologies which send information to you spontaneously, based on pre-arranged parameters that define the things that you are interested in. It's a bit like a radar system that steers your fishing boat to the waters where the fish are.

In the old days a company's internal information services often consisted of little more than a couple of people reading the newspapers, cutting out relevant articles and then filing them away. It was not their responsibility to ensure that relevant people in the organisation were aware of the fact that they were there.

Such a set-up is not unknown today. But it will need to be changed quickly because companies' success will increasingly depend on their ability to see what is coming—not only before it comes, but also before their rivals see it coming.

At Andersen Consulting we have a number of groups devoted to the business of gathering and disseminating information—or, rather, devoted to the business of gathering information and of disseminating intelligence, processing the information en route so that it is presented intelligently to those people who need it. A small group of people, for instance, is continually on the lookout for things that might affect the scenarios we have drawn up for the future of the financial services industry. The group produces a monthly publication called *nEWSletter*, the EWS standing for Early Warning Signals, things which suggest that one scenario is unfolding rather than any other.

Another group, called CSTaR, employs ten full-time staff. They explore the Internet, monitor the output of research companies, scan all the world's newspapers, and do their own research. They focus on things that relate specifically to Andersen Consulting and its clients, which is inevitably quite heavily slanted towards technology. Their key findings are assembled into a report that they produce once a week. Called (significantly) *To the Point*, it is distributed electronically, and every issue is read by about 11,000 employees.

Such large-scale formal scanning systems may not be appropriate for every company. But every company needs something, tailored to meet its particular requirements. The frequency and circulation of regular reports, for instance, will depend very much on the nature of the organisation's business. Some businesses move faster than others. In the IT world things change more rapidly than in the world of shipbuilding.

As the scenarios shift, of course, so do the strategies that go with them. No company should imagine that once it has been through a long period of scenario planning, it can close the book because it will have found a strategy to steer it for the next x number of years. Such an attitude is dangerous; companies can quite easily (and blamelessly) start heading up a strategic cul-de-sac. In many cases it may not be immediately obvious that the cul-de-sac has no exit. Only after taking a turning some way down the road may the driver become aware that there is no way out.

Continuous monitoring of the environment, of the scenarios,

and of strategy itself should become embedded into a company's culture. And as such it should become part of a company-wide process of continuous learning. In today's business world, being able to pick up information quickly and to understand its significance more rapidly than rival firms is a major part of competitive advantage.

The more time we spend absorbing raw data, the less time we have to analyse that data, and it is the analysis which counts in a competitive marketplace. Even the CIA spends most of its time today talking about the implications of information, much of which is in the public domain, rather than getting out and about on the ground (or in a parked car, more likely) sleuthing for facts. The latter, of course, is probably closer to the image that most of us have of what the CIA is about.

Today there are facts galore. In the recent law suits with the tobacco industry in America, the equivalent of some 40,000 legal documents were made available instantly on the Internet, documents that revealed some of the tobacco industry's most intimate secrets. If you're a company that is affected by the tobacco industry, you may be very glad to have access to these documents. But who in your business is going to be delegated to make sense of them and to think about how they apply to you? And how long have they got?

Injecting outside insights

A final 'no brainer' course of action that companies can follow safely is to be more open to people and ideas from other industries and from other countries. In a world where almost all businesses are becoming more and more global, and where industries cross over into each other's territories more and more, it has to be a good idea to recruit people who have experience of different parts of the world and of other businesses.

In any case, knowledge is a key asset everywhere. And knowledge from outside your business or market can be as valuable as that from within.

There are a number of striking examples of managers successfully crossing such borders. Examples in England include the chief executive of Abbey National, a diversified financial services firm, who once sold razor blades. The chief executive of Barclays Bank, Martin Taylor, used to be a journalist on the *Financial Times*, as did John Gardiner, long-time head of the Laird shipping group. The boss of a small award-winning building society, Birmingham Midshires, came from Citibank where he worked for a number of years in California. In his early business life he worked for the aerospace company Hawker Siddeley.

In Australia the financial services industry has also been keen to bring in outsiders. The chief executive of AMP is an American, as is the head of National Australia Bank.

Sometimes outsiders bring teams with them to ensure that their new business gets imbued with their culture rather than the other way round. The ex-Citibanker who went to Birmingham Midshires did just that.

Introducing outsiders is especially important in industries such as banking where the traditional recruitment policy has, for time immemorial, been to employ people as school-leavers and to give them a 'job for life'. When the same people with the same training and the same outlook work together day-in, day-out over a prolonged period of time, they inevitably reinforce each other's prejudices—including the idea that there is no better way of doing things than the way they are (and always have been) done. A strong company culture is only a good thing for as long as it is the right culture for the times. And almost the only way it can be changed is by the introduction of a strong outside influence.

The change introduced by outsiders does not have to be blatant and revolutionary. At Barclays, for instance, Martin Taylor has in a subtle way succeeded in switching the management's prime focus from the quantity of assets to the quality of those assets.

On occasions, it is possible for firms to introduce outsiders from within. Take, for example, the case of Sir John Harvey-Jones. When he was appointed chief executive of ICI, Britain's leading company at the time, he wore big floral ties and had long shaggy hair. If he thought people were getting complacent he would inject an artificial crisis into the business to jolt them out of it.

He was very different from his traditionalist predecessors and from his internal rivals for the job. The board, unable to recruit from outside, had the vision to see that he might provide the company with exactly the breath of fresh air that it needed. Harvey-Jones completely vindicated their choice, and became the classic case of an inside 'outsider'.

For similar reasons, we have found that it is valuable when setting out on a scenario-planning exercise to seek the help of an outside 'facilitator'. Andersen Consulting uses a facilitator in its own scenario-planning exercises. Such a person is able to bring two things in particular to the table—one, the experience of other such planning exercises, and two, the ability to say things like 'that's crazy' to whoever is involved.

We have also found that, in general, there are two main types of facilitator: one sets out the methodology and then tells the group to get on with it. For the rest of the time, they are there to answer questions, but they do not actively participate in the process. The second type of facilitator does just that, getting involved and adding information and ideas at all stages of the scenario planning.

Peter Schwartz of Global Business Network (GBN) is very much the second type of facilitator. But GBN limits its involvement with its clients to the scenario forming process itself. Others continue to work with clients afterwards, advising them on the steps that the scenario planning process has suggested that they take—'getting wet' in various areas, for example, or setting up systems that enable the firm to continue updating and reassessing its scenarios.

The introduction of an outside facilitator can have a dramatic effect. I remember one occasion in South Africa when a leading financial services company invited me to make a presentation of our scenarios for the financial services industry. The chairman began the two-day conference by laying out the company's general strategy for the future, which was essentially one of *laissez faire*.

During my presentation, later that day, I could see him getting a little worried. After my presentation the audience broke up into small discussion groups which a colleague and I facilitated. They became very lively as we started to explore the different scenarios. When they overran their time, the chairman insisted that they continue. Later that day he came up to me, cursed me (in Afrikaans), and said that he was literally in the process of tearing up the corporate strategy having only announced it that morning, based on what he had heard and seen that day!

The presentation and discussion had convinced him that many of the things that he had thought would come to pass were, in fact, very unlikely. It sounds dramatic, but all I had done was to sow the seeds of doubt in his mind. For many companies that is all that is required to spur them to think differently about their future.

At Andersen Consulting we get increasingly involved in drawing up specific scenarios for client companies. The scenarios we have devised ourselves provide a start by giving each company a framework in which to think about its own future. And we have found that our scenarios have considerable durability. Some three years after we designed the ones for the financial services industry they still hold up very well. And financial services is not a business that has stood still in the meanwhile.

Some companies try to instil our scenarios into all their senior managers. At Australia's AMP, for instance, everybody who is hired above a certain management level automatically goes through Andersen Consulting's scenarios for the future of financial services.

Destination Z

One 'user-friendly' way in which managers can be introduced to scenarios is through a game that we have devised at Andersen Consulting. Called Destination Z, it can be played by representatives of a company who want to engage in a structured debate about the future. The game is described in the appendix that follows this chapter.

In our experience there are few top executives who do not admit, after having played the game, that it was a powerful experience. It includes viewing a video in which the players are introduced to the individual scenarios that are shown as if they have really come to pass. The game aims to make people realise that the unbelievable can happen. Who would have thought, for instance, that someone could rise from total obscurity to be the richest man in the world in fewer than 15 years?

The game has been devised to give people a chance to think, however briefly, of what might be the consequences for their business if so-and-so should come about. For, in today's business world, the one thing that is not in surplus is time. As the late Sir James Goldsmith once put it: 'When you see a bandwagon rolling it's already too late to jump on it.'

There is, unfortunately, no more difficult time to persuade people to change than when things are going well. Imagine how hard it must be for a company that is making bumper profits to to its shareholders and tell them: 'We have just embarked on this expensive experiment in a totally new business because we think there is a possibility that the business we are currently doing so well in might not exist in five years' time.' But that is the reality of business today.

Destination Z has been developed by western businessmen with western businesses in mind, but it seems to apply equally well all over the world, even in the Orient where attitudes to time and the whole concept of planning are very different. After all, one of our scenarios is called Keiretsu Rising, a keiretsu being an existing form of Japanese structure. So embedded is it already in Japanese industry that it may be more difficult for a Japanese businessman to conceive of its direct opposites than it is for an American.

But in Japan, long-term planning is something of a national speciality. Companies there think in terms of 50 years rather than five, and if they were to play Destination Z they might want to impose longer time horizons than a US quoted company whose concerns stretch little further than next quarter's results. It is remarkable, for example, to read Sony's mission statement. Written about 50 years ago, it is still eminently suitable today as the philosophy that drives the company.

How will the Japanese cope in a more dynamic world where time is more of the essence? Will they also become more hurried and short-termist as their stock market becomes more like those in the west in demanding short-term results? Or will they maintain their old ways and fall behind in the global race for economic growth?

The answers to these intriguing questions may yet prove to be full of surprises. For the Japanese are as capable as anybody of adapting their behaviour to the needs of the occasion. Who would have imagined that a Japanese bank would go bankrupt (as happened recently) or, even more surprisingly, that the government would let it? And who would have imagined that Japanese companies would lay off workers in the way that they have done recently?

In the rest of Asia it is another story. Places such as Singapore have been much quicker to change. Today there is no more 'wired' society in the world than the island state at the foot of the Malaysian peninsula: the level of automation at the docks there enables ships to turn around cargoes with a speed unmatched anywhere. Yet in Singapore it is ethnic Chinese who make up a large majority of the population, and their fellow Chinese elsewhere have not historically been credited with moving at the speed of light. It is not too hard to believe that the Japanese can adapt too.

In Destination Z players are compelled to decide in what sort of business world they think they will have to operate in the future. Will it be a world like Singapore's, or will it be more like Japan's? Will it be a product-oriented world, or one in which consumers increasingly want a say in the design and production of the goods and services that they buy? If the former, then where on the value chain should they place themselves? On a narrow part of it? Or across a broad canvas?

We can all see that progressive companies such as Levi's are moving into customising jeans and making them 'on demand' rather than 'supplying' them from the end of a production line and hoping that they will then be sold. Likewise, BMW can boast that hardly any two of its cars are identical. But how successful are these companies in pursuing these new and strategically significant directions? How many customised jeans is Levi's actually selling compared with the number it continues to sell 'off the shelf'. Are these just experiments at the margin? Or are they the forerunners of the future? The truth is, it's hard to tell.

Yet on the answers to these and similar questions hang the future of whole companies. Going one way or the other is a big decision. It involves a major investment to retool and customise production in the way that BMW is beginning to do. Do you make that investment now? Or do you wait for further confirmation that customers do in fact want to be more involved in the products that they buy?

At the end of the day the route followed is likely to be a mix of the two—of customisation and of commoditisation. Banks, for example, will have to mix a service for the high net worth individual, who wants personal attention and investment advice, with one for those people whose earnings go into their account one day and almost completely disappear out of it the next.

Looking along the other axis on the board—the 'owner/specialist' axis—we find again that the world is inconveniently neither black nor white; in many industries the signals suggest that a number of different scenarios are being played out simultaneously. Take, for example, the recent spate of American banking industry mergers. The Citicorp/Travellers get-together suggests that the banking world is moving towards the 'owner' end of the axis. Here is a giant combination that can provide a very wide range of commodity-type services across a very wide swathe of the globe. If anything indicates that the world is moving in the direction of the Acme & Co scenario then this, surely, must be it.

But the Citicorp/Travellers deal was followed shortly after by the merger between First Chicago and BancOne of Columbus, Ohio. Though also very big, this merger has a rather different rationale. It is part of a trend towards the formation of super-regional institutions whose aim is to be a specialist in supplying services to customers in a particular region of the United States. In this case it is the grain-growing region that sweeps west from Ohio and through Illinois.

This sort of discussion, and the insights that it leads to, is what the game is all about. But remember that it is not the end of the process, but only the beginning. There is a long journey to be undertaken thereafter as the players attempt to integrate their strategy with their new insights, and as they update their scenarios and their strategies to take relevant changes into account. In the words of the old cliché, their journey is sure to be long and it is sure to be 'a bit of a roller-coaster'. But, as with any roller-coaster, the important thing is to learn to enjoy the ride.

Chapter summary

In this chapter I consider those actions that companies can take immediately after they have been through the scenario planning process.

I have divided these 'no-brainer' actions into five:

✦ First, I consider the need for companies to make themselves more flexible. There are two aspects to this: one is for them to thin down, to streamline themselves so that there is no surplus fat; and the other is for them to take decisions rapidly. This is largely a question of stripping away unnecessary hierarchy and giving people the information that they need for them to make informed decisions quickly.

✦ Secondly, I emphasise the need for companies to 'get wet', to try things out in a way that involves more than merely 'putting a toe in the water'. They need to immerse themselves fully in those new businesses (or new ways of working) that they have identified as potentially significant for them. We refer to the way in which banks have only recently begun to get properly wet with Internet-based services. Nobody can yet tell whether Internet banking is going to be big in the future. But, if it is, then those institutions that have done something substantive with it will be first off the mark when it takes off. Those that have not got wet will be left standing. Likewise with alliances.

Companies need to experiment by forming alliances across industries and across borders. If alliances prove to be the best way for companies to benefit from the way in which the business environment unfolds, then those that have had wide experience with them will be best placed. We emphasise that making alliances work is not easy. Firms need all the practice that they can get.

✦ The third point I make is that companies need to gain a thorough understanding of what their core competencies are. For only when they possess such an understanding can they know what they should specialise in (if a 'specialist' world evolves) or what they need to buy to complement their existing activities (if an 'owner' world evolves).

✦ The fourth point I make is that scenarios are living things that need almost continuous attention. The facts and assumptions that we feed into them are changing all the time. The Pentagon keeps updating its scenarios—and if it feels the need to do so, then so should everyone else. In order to do that companies need to set up sophisticated systems for monitoring and analysing information. The type of system they need depends largely on the type of business that they are in.

✦ Finally, I suggest that all companies can benefit from an injection of outside influence. This means employing people who come from different backgrounds—from different industries, different cultures, different work environments, etc. Only outsiders can steer a company away from a blinkered vision of the future.

Most companies' vision is blinkered in some way—by scarcely recognised prejudices (for example, 'the Chinese don't drink milk, so how can we ever sell them ice cream'), or through years of attempting to placate an overbearing chief executive. The company that is going to survive is the one which is aware that its view is blinkered, and which is prepared to try and do something about it.

I then suggest that readers who have reached this stage of the book should engage their colleagues in an open debate about the future of their company. One such way would be to create their own scenarios; another would be to play a game like Destination Z, which is described more fully in the following appendix.

As Spock used to say in that immortal TV series *Star Trek*, 'Live long and prosper'.

Appendix A

Destination Z: The Game

THIS APPENDIX DESCRIBES IN MORE DETAIL THE BOARD GAME, Destination Z, that we developed in order to help companies devise strategies for their future. Originally designed for the financial services industry, the game can be applied right across the industrial spectrum. Some companies have found it so useful that they have integrated it into their wider strategy-setting process.

Destination Z is a board game that bears some resemblance to Diplomacy. It requires the participation of all the individuals within a firm who are concerned with planning and strategy formulation. Players need to allocate a set period of time for the game, and that must include adequate time for preparation. Like Diplomacy, Destination Z cannot be finished in a day.

To play the game you need a table on which to lay out what we call the Destination Z grid. The grid consists of what by now is the familiar two-by-two matrix. The two axes, representing consumers and suppliers, intersect in the middle, and they stretch (for consumers) from 'co-producer' at one end to 'buyer' at the other; and (for suppliers) from 'owner' at one end to 'specialist' at the other (Figure A1).

Each axis is divided into six segments (Figure A2), with each segment representing a distinct transition, e.g. from a product buyer to a solution buyer. Although each segment is of equal length on the board each one does not necessarily represent the same degree of change. Rather like an underground map, our grid

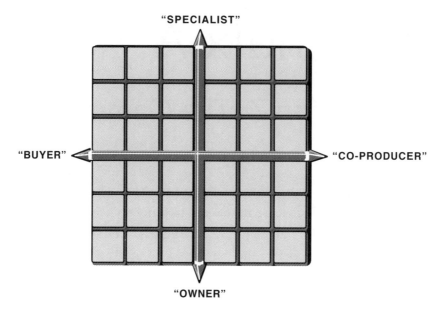

Figure A1   Destination Z grid

gives no indication of distance or effort involved in getting from
one segment to another. The horizontal (consumer) axis has six
segments representing (from left to right):

✦ Commodity buyer;
✦ Product buyer;
✦ Solution buyer;
✦ Solution definer;
✦ Solution co-designer;
✦ Solution co-producer.

The vertical (supplier) axis also has six segments, representing
(from top to bottom):

- ✦ Value network specialist;
- ✦ Value network participant;
- ✦ Value chain participant;
- ✦ Value chain partner;
- ✦ Value chain controller;
- ✦ Value chain owner.

This grid is laid out on a large board which needs to be placed on a high table in the middle of a room—a bit like a wartime operations centre! Large chequer-like pieces are made available to represent competitors as well as the company playing the game. This set-up should make it easy for discussion to begin and for everyone to be engaged in it. The room should not contain any chairs; if participants want to sit down and relax, they can go elsewhere. But the room should contain two or three large white

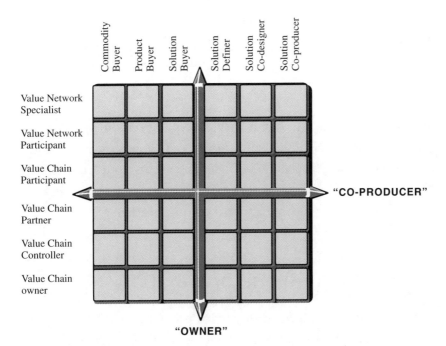

Figure A2   Naming each segment

boards (or, if these are not available, three or four flip charts with adequate wall space where full pages can be affixed). These are needed to record the comments and ideas that arise during the game (and you can be sure that there will be plenty). You want to be certain that nothing is lost from the discussion that will inevitably be stimulated by the game.

The game is designed to help answer four fundamental questions about a business:

1   'Where are we now?' This means drawing a picture of where the organisation and its industry are today.
2   'Where do we need to be in x years' time?' This involves identifying where the organisation thinks it should be at some time in the future—'Destination Z'.
3   'What do we need to do get there?' This is a question of identifying the means needed to reach the destination where the business wants to be in the future.
4   'How do we do what has to be done?' This is a question of focusing on the specific actions needed in order to reach that destination.

It is not a good idea to begin with everybody standing around the game discussing 'Where are we now', and trying to decide where on the board to place the piece that represents your business. At this stage, the board's grid should merely act as a framework for general preparatory debate about the four questions.

Pre-game preparation

The main objective of the period of preparation is to bring out into the open the thoughts and views of all those individuals who are to participate in the game. Only when there is complete openness among the members of the team can the company hope to determine its position (and the positions of its competitors) on the game's board.

As part of the pre-game preparation, each participant must sit down and think about the firm's environment, the firm itself, and its competitors. The aim is for each individual to have a clear personal view of where the firm is now, and (more importantly) where he or she thinks that it should seek to be in the future. Participants should try to free themselves as much as possible from the realities of today's business world.

+ **The firm's environment**. Each player should draw his or her own picture of the environment in which their company is operating. They should concentrate on the political, economic, social and technological influences within that environment, and under each category players should highlight those issues that may have an impact on the firm— both as opportunities and as threats.

+ **The firm**. Having assessed the environment and the factors within it that may be important, players should then consider the strengths and weaknesses of their own firm in relation to each factor. They should set this within the framework of competition devised by Michael Porter of the Harvard Business School. In this, competition between firms takes place at many different points along the 'value chain' by which raw materials are converted into finished products in the hands of consumers. Assess the power of your suppliers and of your customers, and think about whether there are any substitutes for your products.

+ **Your competitors**. Think about who are your firm's competitors, and about what they are doing. What is the level of inter-firm rivalry? And is there a threat of new entrants into your industry? If you have enough time, think about each of your firm's rivals in much the same way as you have thought about your own firm.

While going through this process, it is important that participants record their thoughts. The idea is that each participant should have a clear picture of where their firm is at the present time— before they move on to the interactive part of the game. Time well spent at this stage will make the rest of the game significantly more rewarding.

Where are we now?

Players now come together around the board and try to get each individual's picture of the firm's position to gel into a consensus view. As far as the game is concerned, the aim is to be able to place the company (and its competitors) on a particular square on the board. The wider aim is to get executives to participate in an open and free discussion.

Figure A3   A game in motion

The accuracy with which the company is placed (Figure A3), and the overall value of playing the game, will depend to a large extent on the quality of the questions asked by the participants, and on the ensuing discussion.

At this stage, players should spend some four to six hours considering everyone's point of view about the company and its competitors. The discussion should be structured in the same way as the individuals' own private consideration of the issues.

Ten key questions that the players should be asking themselves at this stage are:

✦ What threats exist in your industry, and how are you currently positioned to handle them?
✦ What resources does your firm have, and are you making the best use of them?
✦ Could a new entrant coming into your industry radically alter it?
✦ What are your competitors currently doing, and how might they change?
✦ What is the propensity of consumers to buy substitutes for your products?
✦ How price sensitive are your customers?
✦ What is the nature of the demand for your product?
✦ How reliant are you on your suppliers and buyers?
✦ Which of them has the dominant power?
✦ What new opportunities exist for your firm?

At the end of this discussion, participants should have reached a consensus on the current position, strategic intent and capabilities of their firm, and of their major competitors. If the process has been particularly successful players might also have identified potential new market entrants and new market opportunities.

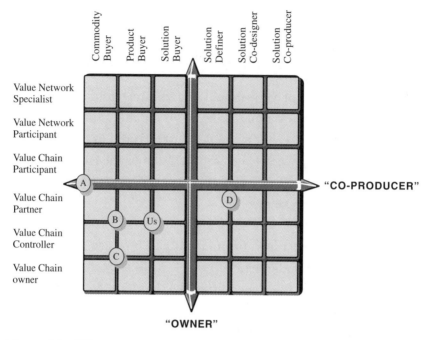

Figure A4   Where are we now

By now the game's board will now have some pieces on it (Figure A4): there will be a green one to indicate the position of the participants' firm, and there will be some yellow ones to indicate where their competitors lie.

Where do we need to be in x years?

The objective at this stage of the game is to decide where on the board you should locate Destination Z. Initially, you need to decide the sort of time frame in which you want to set your future horizons. We have found that a destination between three and ten years hence is the ideal. Such a date is not so far ahead that you begin to think of far-fetched possibilities (factories on Mars, for example, or the turning into desert of large parts of the earth's surface); but at the same time it is not so immediate that it leaves no space for the imagination to wander.

The exact duration will vary according to the industry in which the players are involved. If it is a dynamic fast-changing industry (telecoms, for instance) than a shorter duration will be appropriate. If it is a more mature stable business (detergents, perhaps) then it may be more helpful to think of a longer time frame.

Ultimately the answer to the question 'Where is Destination Z?' will be a combination of the answers to two other questions:

✦ What would you like your firm to be doing in x years' time?
✦ And what will the environment—and your competitors— actually allow you to do in that time frame?

The answer to the first question should not be too hard to find, and it should help your organisation to define its strategic intent. The answer to the second question, however, will be more difficult, and you will need to make use of all the information that you have generated during the earlier stages of the game to come up with an honest answer.

If all is well, the answers to the two questions will be the same. If they're not, then you might have to make some painful adjustment to your ambitions for the firm.

If the early stages progress smoothly you should be able to identify Destination Z within another three to four hours; if all goes very well then you might also have been able to identify the Destination Zs of some of your firm's rivals during the same time. By the end of this stage you will have been able to add at least one more piece to the board—the one marked Destination Z (Figure A5). With luck, you will also have been able to add some pieces representing the desired destinations of your rivals.

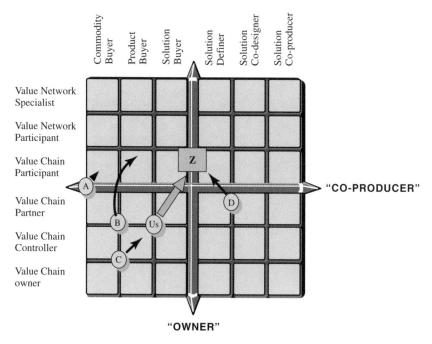

Figure A5   Where do we need to be

What do we need to do?

In this part of the process participants attempt to identify what they need to do in order to take the right steps towards Destination Z, the steps that they can now see from their board are necessary if they are to move from where they are now to there. This can be a daunting process, and it is recommended that at least four hours be set aside for it so that everyone's opinion can be heard.

There are many questions whose answers will have a bearing on the conclusion that the players reach. For example:

✦ What must we do with our products?
✦ Do we need to build alliances, merge and/or absorb other firms?

✦ Do we need to globalise our operations?

✦ Do we need to outsource, and if so, what?

✦ Will our competitors seek the same destination? And if the answer is 'yes', do we need to try and stop them reaching it, or just ensure that we get there first?

✦ If getting to Z first is essential, then how can we best deploy our current capabilities to achieve this?

✦ Should we concentrate on trying to create technological advances internally?

The aim is to devise the tactics that you will need to employ at a macro level in order to take your firm to its own Destination Z. At the end of this stage players should have a clear series of tactics that they believe will take them to their chosen destination.

How do we do it?

In this final stage, players aim to identify the ways in which they will need to change the firm in order to reach Destination Z, and what they can do to build a management consensus in favour of those changes. Again this will take some time, and between four and six hours should be set aside for the initial discussion.

This discussion should start at a basic level with an analysis of the firm's resources and capabilities. We recommend that this follow the framework devised by Robert Grant in which resources are divided into two types: tangible resources, such as physical assets and financial assets; and intangible resources, things such as human resources, technological resources, the firm's reputation, and the skills that it retains. Grant wrote *Contemporary Strategy Analysis*, published 1991, Blackwells.

As far as the tangible assets are concerned, there are only two important questions:

+ What opportunities exist for economising on their use?
+ And what possibilities exist for employing them more profitably?

With the intangible assets, the key is to gain a clear picture of what they are and of their strengths. Then players need to go on to find ways in which they can be leveraged so that they help the firm to progress to its destination. Grant suggests that each identified resource be assessed in terms of four qualities: its appropriability, its durability, its transferability, and its replicability.

Once this has been completed, players will have a good idea of what needs to be done to their firm's resources in order to start on their journey to Destination Z. As part of this process they will consider how their distribution channels, suppliers and customers will react to their actions. But they should also remember that an important issue is always: 'How will my competitors react to my chosen tactics?' They should consider this carefully before concluding this stage.

After that, players can relax for a while before they start the really hard work—communicating the changes needed to others, and gathering a consensus across the firm as it embarks on what will probably become a major programme of change.

One final word of warning, however. Further unanticipated changes are bound to take place over time, and these might shift the position on the board of your Destination Z and the path you need to take to reach it. We therefore recommend that firms dedicate time at regular intervals to playing the game again . . . and again . . .

Index